POSITIVE STRESS MANAGEMENT

POSITIVE
STRESS
MANAGEMENT

A PRACTICAL GUIDE
FOR THOSE WHO
WORK UNDER PRESSURE

PETER E MAKIN · PATRICIA A LINDLEY

**KOGAN
PAGE**

First published in 1991

Kogan Page Limited
120 Pentonville Road
London N1 9JN

British Library Cataloguing in Publication Data

A CIP record for this book is available from the British Library.

ISBN 0–7494–0342–X

Typeset by DP Photosetting, Aylesbury, Bucks
Printed and bound in Great Britain by
Clays Ltd, St Ives plc

Contents

CHAPTER 1
Introduction

You don't have to be stressed to read this book!

In fact, the book was written as much for people who want to take positive action in managing their lives, as for people who want to learn how to cope with pressure.

You don't have to read the book straight through, cover to cover, to find the bits relevant to you. There is a questionnaire on pages 15–18. The remaining chapters each cover one area of self-management. You can use the questionnaire to get a feel for what is covered by each chapter and then turn directly to the ones that are most relevant to you. Before you begin this, however, please take five minutes to read over hints and tips on how to make the most of this book (see below). Most of us read in such a casual way that we fail to get full value out of material we study. Just using a few of the tips will give you a more worthwhile return on the time and energy you spend reading.

Ten suggestions to help you to get the most out of this material

1. The first point is to *deliberately set out to learn*. We often read in rather a casual way (for example, how much can you remember from yesterday's paper?). It takes a special effort to consciously try to learn; to identify ideas that we might use and then work these into our everyday routine. Research shows that this is exactly what effective learners do: they set out to learn and they use every way they know how to help them to learn.

2. The second point is to *be selective*. This book is full of ideas to help you to manage stress. Although we have tried to limit the number of ideas included, there is still a lot of material here. Only some of this material is likely to be relevant to you at this moment.

   Concentrate on one key point rather than a dozen general ideas. Take what you want and put the rest to one side, ready for when you might want it in the future.

3. *Read with a pencil and paper handy*, otherwise you are putting an unnecessary burden on your memory. When you see an important point, underline it or put a mark in the margin. The material in this book will be of little worth if you can't highlight the bits you find useful.

   As well as highlighting text, jotting down notes of your own is an excellent way to support your learning. This may sound an obvious point but you only need to see how many books fail to leave any space for readers' notes to realise how often it is overlooked. In this book we have allocated space for your notes at various points throughout the text. Even if you don't write in these spaces, use them as a signal to stop reading for a minute and reflect on the text you have just covered. These periods of reflection are often the times we learn the most.

   Another way to make more of your notes is to pin up any really good points in a place where you will see them regularly, or to reserve a special page for them in your diary.

4. *Start with your top priority*. If you do not know your top priority, think about the kind of pressure you are under at work and the sort of things you worry about. Ask yourself in what ways you would have to be different (eg healthier, more relaxed, more assertive) in order to cope with these things. List the three major differences. These are your three top priorities and you should work on them first.

> My priorities: the three major changes I would like to see in myself:
>
> 1.
>
> 2.
>
> 3.

5. *Keep an open mind.* This is easy to say but can be all too difficult to do. Edward de Bono, one of the world's leading experts in creative thinking, has devoted much of his work to this one issue. The key is to suspend judgement on an idea while you explore its possibilities.

   Try to do this when you go through the ideas here. If you see an idea that you like but which you think is impractical, try to look for reasons why you *can* use that idea rather than reasons why you can't.

6. *Start with the least difficult change* you would like to make and work upwards. The purpose of doing things this way is that you are more likely to succeed if you have set reasonable goals. Setting impossible targets is just a way of setting up failure.

7. *Record your progress and reward your success.* One good reason for starting with the least difficult change is that you are in the running for a reward. If you set up a major test as a starter, then you are odds *against* a reward. You are also likely to have to wait a long time. In stress management, we want to monitor behaviour on a daily and weekly basis and allocate rewards on a daily and weekly basis. These rewards truly reflect behaviour. Giving ourselves an extra holiday next year does not reward behaviour today.

   Don't think of a reward as just a packet of sweets – or even a bottle of champagne. You reward yourself with whatever you find enjoyable or desirable. If it helps, make a list of possible rewards now.

_____

_____

_____

Pick an appropriate reward in advance for a particular project and work towards it. Then you can take great pleasure in giving it to yourself when the time comes.

8. *Learn by your mistakes.* Recent research shows that rather than becoming disillusioned by their mistakes, effective learners use these errors to help them learn. This is what scientific experimentation is all about. Edison recognised this during his work on the light bulb. After 10,000 unsuccessful experiments he was asked if he felt disillusioned. He replied that he did not, since he had succeeded 10,000 times in finding out what not to do.

To use your mistakes to help you learn, simply ask (1) 'What did I do wrong?' and (2) 'What should I do next time?' Write down your thoughts as a way of keeping a record of your learning points.

9. *Apply what you learn.* Research shows that new behaviour is more likely to stay in our repertoire if we try it out soon after learning it. If you are unable to practise something immediately, then spend a few minutes pondering how you might use it in the future. This pondering is an important part of learning – try it as a review on any occasion. To ponder, ask yourself, 'What can I learn from this? How can I use this learning in the future?'

If you are unable to practise something immediately, you may find it helpful to jot down exactly what it is you have learned. You don't need to write much – just get down the key point. Then spend a few minutes pondering how you might use this learning in the future. Plan out any action you will take. To help you do this planning we have provided a

Personal Planner page near the end of each chapter. We hope you will use these Personal Planners throughout the book and go on to apply the same idea to learning experiences in your everyday life.

10. *Get support.* Stress management is about supporting yourself – supporting yourself in the way you assess your performance in something, in how you think and how you behave.

    But there is also the support of others. In learning, other people are about the most valuable support you can find. Try to find just one person who you can share your learning with. Ask him or her if they would mind being your 'learning partner' and explain how you would like this to work. If there is no one person you can think of, then why not have several 'learning partners', each for a separate area?

People I can use as learning partners:

People   **How they could help me**

1. _____   _____

                             _____

2. _____   _____

                             _____

3. _____   _____

                             _____

Summary

1. Deliberately set out to learn.
2. Be selective.
3. Keep a pencil and paper handy.
4. Start with your top priority.
5. Keep an open mind.
6. Start with the easiest thing to change – set yourself up for success.
7. Record your progress and reward your successes.
8. Learn by your mistakes.
9. Ponder what you learn and use this learning as soon as possible.
10. Get support. Find and use a learning partner or partners.

CHAPTER 2
You, Pressure and Performance

A quick introduction to stress and pressure

What makes us stressed?

Many things can make us stressed. A car coming towards us at high speed, for example, or the prospect of a difficult meeting with senior management. Stress is the response to the pressure we feel in these situations. Certain amounts of pressure provide healthy stimulus but too much or too little pressure can lead to stress.

How much pressure we feel depends on us and how we see the situation, not the situation itself. Epictetus wrote, 'People are disturbed not by things but by the view they take of them.' We are likely to feel stressed when we perceive a mismatch between what we see as our abilities and what we see as the demands of the situation.

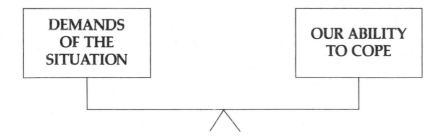

What does stress do to you physically?

The physical stress response is purely and simply that of the body gearing up for immediate action. Triggered by the hypothalamus in the brain, the body automatically:

- releases adrenalin into the bloodstream (for energy)
- shuts down the digestive system
- thickens blood so that it will clot if you are cut
- pumps blood around the body to muscles and essential organs

(The physical stress response is explained in more detail in Chapter 6 on page 85.)

The purpose of having this instant, automatic response is to save time: if you had to think about your reaction it would take too long. If you have ever had to jump out of the way of an approaching car you will appreciate just how quickly the body can work.

The problem with the stress response is that physical reaction (ie fight or flight) is not always the appropriate way of handling today's problems. Many of today's pressures really don't require a *physical* response at all. Running a meeting, for example, requires calm and control; the physical stress response is no help at all.

How long does stress last?

The stress response was designed to be short-lived. It provides a quick burst of energy, a bit like jumping on the accelerator in a car. This is fine as long as there is time to recover between one stressful event and the next.

However, in today's increasingly fast-moving world, stressful situations can follow in quick succession, leaving us continually in a state of somewhat heightened arousal. This state can feel unpleasant psychologically and lead to our becoming more irritable and prone to errors. It can also be physically harmful if the stress response remains elevated for too long. Physical consequences include skin disorders, stomach complaints, headaches and muscular tension.

Your pressure profile: what to start on first

It is for you to choose the area you most need to develop. To help you make this choice:

- Complete the self-assessment questionnaire items on the following pages. These items will help you to identify the things that cause you pressure and will highlight the part of the book that will be most relevant to you.

- Try thinking of the kinds of situation in which you tend to feel pressured. Look at the contents list and see if your area features there.

Self-assessment questionnaire

Read through the questionnaire and tick either 'Yes' or 'No' in answer to each item.

Section 1	**YES**	**NO**
Do you often find that you:		
1. Are late for appointments?		☑
2. Stay late at work for an hour or more to finish something?		☑
3. Cancel social engagements or leisure activities in favour of work?		☑
4. Have to work in a rush at the last minute to meet a deadline?		☑
5. Set yourself unrealistic deadlines and have to extend time-scales?		☑
6. Are unsure which of your priorities should take precedence?	☑	
7. Fail to make a note of meetings or tasks to be done?	☑	
8. Are busy and overworked, but never seem to get anything finished?		☑

Section 2

	YES	NO

Do you often find that you:

1. Say 'Yes' when you really want to say 'No'? ☑ ☐
2. Don't know how to say what you want to say? ☑ ☐
3. Say 'No' and feel guilty afterwards? ☑ ☐
4. Feel manipulated? ☑ ☐
5. Get emotional when you know you should be stating your views calmly? ☑ ☐
6. Feel embarrassed and unable to admit you don't understand something? ☐ ☑
7. Apologise for saying what you want? ☐ ☑
8. Are unable to ask directly for what you want? ☑ ☑

Section 3

Do you often find that you:

1. Are unnecessarily sharp or irritable with other people? ☐ ☑
2. Take a long time to wind down after a stressful event? ☑ ☐
3. Are unable to switch off at the end of the day? ☑ ☐
4. Have trouble getting a full night's sleep? ☑ ☐
5. Get angry over little things? ☑ ☐
6. Feel excessively 'hyped-up' or on edge? ☐ ☐
7. Become tense before even going into some situations? ☐ ☐
8. Work through the day without a proper break? ☑ ☐

Section 4

	YES	NO

Do you often find that you:

1. Feel tired and listless for no apparent reason? ☐ ☑
2. Have recurrent headaches? ☐ ☑
3. Use drinking or smoking to help you to cope? ☐ ☑
4. Have tense and aching muscles? ☐ ☑
5. Suffer from indigestion? ☐ ☑
6. Rely on numerous cups of strong coffee to keep you going? ☐ ☑
7. Go through a week without taking any physical exercise at all? ☑ ☐
8. Don't have time to eat properly? ☑ ☐

Section 5

Do you often find that you:

1. Allow criticism to get you down? ☑ ☐
2. Feel a lack of confidence in your own ability? ☑ ☐
3. Worry that something will go wrong? ☑ ☐
4. Let small things get you down? ☑ ☐
5. Feel unsure about how good you really are? ☑ ☐
6. Concentrate on what is wrong instead of what is right? ☑ ☐
7. Fail to give yourself credit and reward yourself when things go right? ☑ ☐
8. Fail to spot areas where you might improve? ☑ ☐

Section 6	YES	NO

Do you often find that you:

1. Feel isolated and alone? ☑ ☐

2. Have no one to turn to for practical advice? ☑ ☐

3. Want to manage your life better but don't know where to start? ☑ ☐

4. Feel over-dependent on only one or two other people? ☑ ☐

5. Wish you were more independent and self-sufficient? ☑ ☐

6. Cannot seem to break a habit you would like to lose? ☑ ☐

7. Have no one to turn to for emotional support? ☑ ☐

8. Have nothing much in life other than your work? ☑ ☐

Scoring your responses

Now that you have answered the questionnaire you should be able to select the most relevant starting point for your stress management.

Add up your 'Yes' responses for each section of the questionnaire. Enter these scores in the appropriate boxes on the next page.

Each section of the questionnaire corresponds to one of the remaining six chapters in this book. Therefore you can use your scores on the questionnaire to help you decide which chapter to turn to first.

Section	'Yes' Score	Relevant chapters
1	2	How to organise your work, manage your time and control your life (3)
2	5	How to communicate effectively and assertively (4)
3	7	How to relax before, during and after stress (5)
4	6	How to keep your body healthy and fit to cope with stress (6)
5	8	How to assess your performance accurately, be positive and assume control (7)
6	8	How to build, use and give support (8)

Notes

CHAPTER 3
How to Gain Control of Your Time

In this chapter, you will learn:

- How to be clear about your long-term goals
- How and when to set objectives
- How to decide what to do and what not to do
- How to schedule work
- How to maintain a balance between home and work
- How to stay organised

Ten steps towards gaining control

1. Establish long-term goals first

This is because just being organised on a day-to-day basis is of limited value if you do not know where you are going. Imagine a ship in the same situation: each individual member of the crew could be well organised and proficient but if the overall direction was unclear, no real progress would be made.

If you are not quite sure what it is you want to achieve in the long term, try this: pretend you are a journalist and write your own obituary as you would like it to appear.

To help you, here is an example:

Tom Smith's obituary   *Tom Smith is remembered for his success in blending the three important parts of his life: his career, his family and his concern for the environment. At work he earned the reputation of a manager who kept cool in a crisis and who always had time for his staff. Outside work he managed to reserve time for his family and his voluntary work, making an enthusiastic contribution to local environment groups.*

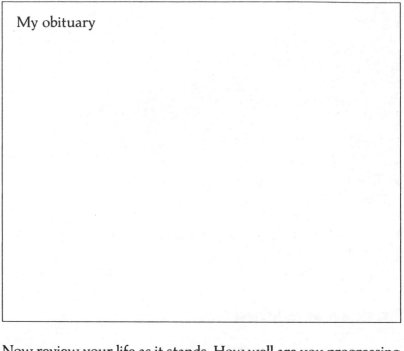

My obituary

Now review your life as it stands. How well are you progressing towards the things you would like to achieve (that is, those things that you have just written about yourself)? What changes in direction do you need to make? As a constant reminder, decide your goals for:

(a) 10 years' time
(b) 5 years' time
(c) this year

and list them prominently in your diary.

2. Look at your goals in terms of behaviour

Ask yourself which of your current behaviour patterns support your progress towards your goals. Which do not support your progress? What behaviour patterns do you need to develop in order to progress towards your goals? As an example here is how Tom Smith might have chosen to develop to reach his long-term goals (those set out in his obituary):

- Start talking to my staff this week – introduce an 'open door' policy.
- Set aside time for my family – two evenings this week.
- Learn to relax and stay calm in crisis situations – seek stress management training.
- Join a local environmental group – pick up forms on Friday.

3. Set objectives at the time-scales critical for you

For example, what do your goals mean in terms of daily, weekly or monthly action? Your own time-scale could mean anything from quarterly reviews to objectives set several times a day. A boxer, for example, may set himself objectives for each new round in a fight. A tennis-player may set a new target for each separate point in a match.

In a business context, this may mean setting objectives for each meeting you attend. A colleague of ours, for example, lists her objectives for all important telephone calls: she lists not just the areas she wants to cover (as many people do) but also what she wants to get out of that call. She is a very successful telephone negotiator.

4. List everything you have to do before you start

Perhaps the simplest thing you can do that will have the most impact on your time is to list everything you have to do before you start. Such 'To do' lists help you to get your bearings. To make the most of your 'To do' list put the items in order of priority. One of the easiest ways of doing this is to classify the items A, B or C. 'A' items are those that have to be done today – the most important; 'B' items are next in importance – the ones you would like to get done; lastly, 'C' items are those that really do not need to be done today. Simply tackle your As first, then your Bs. Only tackle your Cs if you have time left over afterwards.

5. Weigh up the consequences of doing or not doing each task

Most of us do this in other parts of our lives without necessarily realising it, such as when we drive through or stop at a traffic light changing to red. Here, we calculate instantly which is safer – driving on or screeching to a halt. At work you will find that deliberately thinking through the consequences can help you to see what is really important and what can wait.

6. Avoid 'substitute activities'

These are all the things you can contrive to do before settling down to the main task in hand. For example, when at home have you ever said, 'I'll just do the washing up and then I'll ring my mother'?; or at work, 'I'll just tidy the desk first, then I'll write the report.' You probably know what your own 'I'll justs' are, but it is still easy to fool yourself with them because you do achieve *something* – that is, the washing up gets done, the desk is tidied. Unfortunately, the main task has also been successfully delayed (or even avoided). The way to overcome substitute activities is to recognise them for what they are at the outset and *re-substitute* them. Instead of doing them first, mark them down to be done *after* your main task.

Some people are expert at selecting substitute activities and it becomes difficult to know what is a substitute and what a genuine task. If this is true for you, putting your activities into order of priority is all the more important. If all else fails, simply rank your activities in order of importance and do the most important one first.

7. Compile a 'Not to do' list

As well as a 'To do' list, a 'Not to do' list might include, for example:

- *Do not* write budget review – leave it for tomorrow.
- *Do not* attend general management meeting – send Jenkins.
- *Do not* take any phone calls before midday – get secretary to put calls through to Jones.

This immediately cuts out a wide range of activities and allows you to concentrate on those which do need to be done. You will even find that 'Not to do' lists can be a help in pruning over-long 'To do' lists.

8. Compile a 'To do' list at the end of the day

Many people almost certainly write their 'To do' lists first thing in the morning. After all, it makes good sense to clarify at the beginning of the day what you want to achieve during the remainder. But what is wrong with writing a preliminary 'To do' list last thing in the evening, ready for the next day? You can always add to it in the morning. And writing the list in the evening underlines the end of the working day.

Try this and you will find that off-loading work concerns in a list helps you to relax in the evening and sleep more peacefully at night.

'Before I go to bed I make a list of all the things which need doing tomorrow and then try not to think about any of them.'

Anna Massey, award-winning actress

9. Value your time

The purpose behind setting objectives and ranking activities in order is to make more effective use of time. In many ways, the saying 'Time is money' is true: time is often the most valuable currency that we deal in at work. Consider the implications of this in your behaviour. If someone took money from you, or threatened to withhold money due to you, you would probably take immediate action. Is it the same with time? If someone calls round for some of your time, what do you say? How do you handle planning if people try to cut back on the time agreed? If you see time as money, you are far more likely to take a firmer stand on these issues. A firm stand on time can mean an extra hour at the end of the day – an extra hour to finish that report, or the difference between finishing your work at the office or taking it home in the evening.

10. Set aside uninterrupted 'Thinking Time'

Do you sometimes find that, although ideally you would like to plan, you move from crisis to crisis? You really are *too busy* to stop and plan ahead.

If this is true for you, you need to set aside some uninterrupted 'Thinking Time'.

Colonel David Hackworth, the most decorated US soldier in Vietnam, did this. He recognised that most soldiers were 'doers'; this was their strength, but it was also their weakness. They were so busy doing that they never had time to stop and think. Too often, this meant that their constant activity was to little avail – they were running in circles 'chasing their own tails'.

Hackworth's own solution was to set aside a little time for reflection. He found that in this way he was able to capitalise on his past experience; to think through the way he did things and learn from his mistakes so that he could do things differently the next time.

Obviously, Hackworth was operating in the middle of a war zone. He didn't have very much time for reflection but even so he made sure that he had *some* time. Give yourself the same consideration, and make sure your time is uninterrupted: every time you are interrupted you lose not only the interruption time but also the disruption time – the time it takes to get settled afterwards. Interrupted Thinking Time is therefore probably at best 60 per cent efficient. Uninterrupted Thinking Time gives you 100 per cent efficiency.

One way to reduce interruptions is to mark a standard period (say half an hour or an hour) as 'Unavailable Time'. This works well if you balance it with an equal period of 'Available Time', when people know that they *can* get hold of you.

Another way to reduce disturbances is to jot down your daily (or weekly) profile of interruptions. Which are your quietest times? Which your most disturbed? Once you have clarified these, schedule your Thinking Time to take place during your quietest times.

SCHEDULING WORK AND REST TIME AWAY FROM WORK

Holidays and weekends

Managing your time also means building in breaks, setting aside time to recharge your batteries. When we asked Sir John Harvey-Jones, ex-chairman of ICI, what he did to manage pressure in his life, he told us that he kept his weekends sacrosanct. This rule provided him with a reliable break from work every week.

On top of this, he also told us he was 'brutal' with his holidays. He *always* took his holidays. This way he provided his company with a fresh and more effective employee.

If you find yourself working through weekends or missing holidays, then take another look at your planning. You may not be doing your employer any favours in terms of your effectiveness at work and you could be setting a time-bomb for yourself. Take Sir John Harvey-Jones' example: plan some time away from work and make this time sacrosanct.

Breaks and rest periods

Taking breaks is just as important on a small scale. Over 50 years ago, F W Taylor demonstrated that a physical worker can do more work if he or she takes more time off to rest (see Chapter 5 on page 62). The consequences of mental fatigue are just as debilitating as the consequences of physical fatigue, so whether your work is physical or mental, apply this rule: take regular breaks and try to rest *before* you feel tired. If you are not convinced, try it for a day. Schedule regular breaks (however short) and take them. Use them to relax; go for a stroll, or have a chat. But don't do any work. Then return to work and, at the end of the day, check your productivity.

Tom, the manager who abandoned time management

Tom was an effective manager who got fed up with time management. He decided to stop trying to manage his time and to become more spontaneous. He vowed he would take each event as it occurred and try not to calculate when to do such and such or how long this or that task would take. Tom was convinced that his other managerial skills would see him through. He was good at his job, he reasoned, and would not consciously waste time. Indeed, he might even save a few minutes each day on the time he used to spend planning. But he knew that with his new approach he should not even be thinking this way – of the time he could save. Time management was out; he would get on with doing his job.

The first day began well. Tom launched straight into a project that had aroused his interest. True, he was interrupted by other small tasks he could (and should) have put aside, but generally he felt good. It was lunch-time in no time at all.

Tom started again in the afternoon, aware of some other pressing jobs to be done that day. Not unduly concerned, he spent the first hour on the project he had begun in the morning. Then he stopped, a little reluctantly – interesting as the project was, he knew he had all week to complete it. He looked at what he had to do in the rest of the day and was a little alarmed. Maybe he had misjudged things a bit. However, always a man of action, he set to work immediately. The first job he tackled involved telephoning a few colleagues. He was slightly irked to find that three of them who had been in that morning would now be out of the office for two days. He put that job on hold and started the next one. This consisted of putting some figures together for the chairman. He already had the necessary information to work with, so all he would have to do was a bit of calculating and arranging. At 4.30 pm he was still doing this ('Just as bad as last time,' he thought to himself grimly), when an urgent telephone call came through: there was an engineering problem on site. It was the last thing he needed and would rule out any other work that day.

As Tom left for home at 6.00 pm, he pondered on his nonproductive day. 'A bit unlucky,' he said, to encourage himself. But he knew now that he had twice as much to do tomorrow.

By Thursday, Tom was feeling pretty down. Things had gone from bad to worse: unexpected problems had arisen, tasks were taking longer than he anticipated, and he seemed to be spending more time than ever on pointless paperwork (he was even taking some of this home with him now). He now seriously doubted that the project he had begun on Monday could be completed on target tomorrow. He knew that letting the work prey on his mind at home made him more irritable and his wife didn't seem to understand that sometimes work had to come first.

What Tom didn't do

Tom was heading for problems when he didn't:

- Set objectives for the week, as well as for individual tasks (and check whether these objectives fitted in with long-term goals)
- Put activities in order of priority on a day-to-day basis
- Schedule work, bearing in mind all contingencies and previous experience
- Allow time for home as well as work

Try Tom's test on yourself. Have you done all of these this week?

Five points on effective timetabling

1. Ask yourself how much time it will take

Note that this is different from just setting the deadline for a piece of work. For example, imagine you have two jobs to do, both with a deadline of tomorrow lunch-time. If you calculate that each will take a day to complete, you know straight away that the deadlines are unrealistic and you are setting yourself an impossible task. By looking ahead and asking yourself how long the task(s) will take, you are able to anticipate timetabling difficulties before they arise. When you are calculating how long something will take, give it your best estimate and then add a little extra.

'Time taken on a job is always longer than time allowed.'

Anon

2. Be aware of all the things you need to take into account

Timetabling should also involve a systematic check through to see that you have taken everything into account. Without a detailed timetable you can easily be lulled into talking about generalities. Setting yourself the discipline of working out a timetable is an effective way of reassuring yourself and your client or manager that every detail has been considered. One way to help make sure that your timetable does cover everything is to ask yourself at the outset, 'What are all the things I need to take into account?', then make a list. When you draw up your timetable, refer back to this list. It is quite likely that you will find one or two details which you would otherwise have overlooked.

3. Anticipate problems

In a good timetable you should not only consider all the variables, you should also seek to anticipate problems. If you look back at difficulties you have encountered in your career, you will probably find that more than 50 per cent of these could have been predicted. And if you can predict a problem, you can usually plan to avoid it or carry on with contingency plans. For example, if you were driving to a meeting on the other side of London, you might anticipate problems on the M25. As a result you could leave earlier to give yourself a 'time cushion'. You could also check the map for an alternative route in case the traffic is too congested. Finally, you might add some 'unknown' time. Even when you have tried to allow time for problems you have predicted, there can still be possibilities you have not anticipated. Building in unknown or 'fallow' time gives you a further cushion: you will probably be surprised at how often you need it.

'What we anticipate seldom occurs; what we least expect generally happens.'

Benjamin Disraeli

4. Work with your natural rhythms

What does timetabling mean in terms of your daily schedule? Whatever you have to do you will have a preferred pattern of working: you may like frequent short breaks or longer work periods followed by longer breaks; you may be a morning person or an evening person. Try to identify the working pattern that suits you best. Then, as far as you can, tailor your daily schedule to your preferred pattern. The more you work with your natural rhythms, the more productive you are likely to be.

5. Use your schedule, don't let it use you

Schedules are only ways of helping you to achieve a goal – they are not goals in themselves. Overrule your schedule when the situation demands. Some people become stuck in rigid routines which no longer support them, so check your routines and schedules regularly. In general, do they support you? Do they support you for this job? Ask yourself periodically: Why do I do this in this way? Could I do it better another way?

Six further ways to save time and stay organised

1. Keep a problem diary

Note down in your diary when things go wrong and you feel stressed or under pressure. Try to do this regularly after any important piece of work, or spend a few minutes at the end of the day picking out the bad times. Just by doing this exercise you will become more aware of the areas you can improve. And reviewing your problem diary on your own or with your manager is a good way to identify training and development needs.

2. Keep a clear desk

Question the need for anything on your desk that you are not actually using. As a rule of thumb, clear your desk of anything you are not working on. This helps to ensure that you stick to one task at a time. It also engenders a feeling of being organised and in control, whereas an overcrowded desk is an all too painful reminder of everything that has to be done (including those things on your 'Not to do' list).

There are several ways in which you can avoid being smothered in the build-up of paperwork and general clutter. One is to have a 'clear out' day once a month. Mark this in your diary, and on your clear out day go through any paperwork and clutter and challenge its right to be there. An important rule to follow when you do this is not to ask yourself, 'Will I ever need this?' but, 'Will I be able to get this from somebody else, should I need it?' You can usually let somebody else become the hoarder instead of you.

Another way to cut down the paperwork is to apply a 'one touch' rule. How often have you picked up a piece of paperwork and to all intents and purposes 'toyed' with it, before putting it down to come back to it later? Research done in America suggests that some managers will 'bit process' the same piece of paper 12 to 14 times before they finally finish with it. Try to ensure that you have all the time, information and resources for a given piece of paperwork and then apply the one touch rule.

A third way to cut down clutter is to give any paperwork a 'life-time'. Then, processed or not, any given piece of paperwork can be unceremoniously thrown in the bin once its life-time date is up.

3. Write yourself notes

If you don't write notes, you leave the burden on your memory. Put the notes where you are most likely to see them: in your diary, on the car dashboard, by the telephone – any prominent place where they will be noticed.

4. Look out for under-used time

This is any time which is only partly used, like the time spent in a traffic jam, for example. See if you can turn this into 'double time'. Double time is when you use time to do more than one thing: for example, sitting in the car in a traffic jam and listening to a stress management tape; or taking care of some straightforward paperwork while waiting for an imminent telephone call. An often-cited domestic example you can test yourself on is, what do you do while you're waiting for the kettle to boil? There are many times when what we do does not require all our capacity and we can 'double up'. This does not necessarily mean taking on more work. Why not use double time to relax and practise stress management techniques?

5. Challenge interruptions

We have mentioned reducing the number of interruptions by setting yourself some Unavailable Time and requiring your staff and colleagues to filter out low priority items. However, the most important variable in the interruption equation is *your response*. Try challenging the need for the interruption in a fair yet forceful way. There are four particular tactics you can use here.

(a) You can ask the interrupter to *keep to your Available Time* – the time you have set aside for just such matters. Often the interrupter may not have been aware of your Available Time or had forgotten about it. The trick is to stick to the formula so that people become used to the routine.

(b) You can *specify the limits* of your availability. Remember that others are not to know you are busy unless you tell them. If you are unavailable, say so, and say how long you will be held up. If you can spare some time, limit it by defining it. For example, don't say, 'I haven't got long,' but, 'I can give you five minutes,' if that is all you can manage. Then keep to that limit.

(c) You can *give the interrupter alternatives*. Tell people when you will be available. For example, 'I am not free now but I can see you at 2.30 this afternoon or 11.00 tomorrow morning. Which time suits you?' A variant of this, when someone asks for just a few minutes of your time, is, 'I can give you five minutes now or half an hour at 4.30.' Giving alternatives like this leapfrogs any argument over your current availability and starts the interrupter thinking about which other times would be convenient.

(d) You can *state the consequences* of the interruption. This allows the other person to weigh up whether or not the matter is really worth it. This technique is especially useful if you are interrupted by someone senior to you. For example, 'I'm happy to take on the Smith Project, although it will mean letting go of one of my other priorities – which one do you want me to drop?' People have to be clear that if they want your time, there will be consequences.

Challenging interrupters like this is part of being assertive. See Chapter 4 on page 47 for more tips – particularly if you become angry with people who interrupt you or you find it difficult to say 'No'.

6. Challenge your need to attend meetings

We have meetings with other people for good reasons – chiefly to give and receive information. However, meetings, just like anything else, should be subject to your list of priorities. Is attending this meeting more important than the other work you have to do? Is the meeting an A, B or C priority?

The problem is often that, while some points in any given meeting will be relevant to you and a high priority, the rest of the points are irrelevant or unimportant. You can end up wasting half a day for the sake of one 10-minute item. Fortunately, there are two simple tactics that can help you to minimise the impact of this problem.

First, as a rule of thumb, attend only those meetings in which you have an interest in at least 75 per cent of the content. If it is less than this, your time would almost certainly be better spent in your office where you have a 100 per cent stake in what you are doing. Try using this tactic when you invite people to meetings as well. Not only will you cut down the number of meetings but you will also find that the people who do attend will be more motivated, knowing that the content will be relevant to them.

Second, if you do have to attend meetings that breach the 75 per cent rule, ask for permission to leave once your business is concluded. You will usually gain nothing by staying on after this. And as far as everyone else is concerned, there is nothing worse than disinterested people hanging around in meetings to which they no longer have anything to contribute.

Balancing work and home life

Decide on your primary values

You must sort out your values and priorities. If you find it hard to identify your key values immediately, then try this exercise. Which of the following do you value most?

(a) your work
(b) your home/leisure life
(c) your health.

Which of these three is your primary value?

Ask yourself, 'To which of these values do I devote most of my energy?' Now which is your primary value?

Direct your behaviour to support your primary value

If you spend more of your energy on a secondary value it means that, for all intents and purposes, that value is your primary value. The value you support by your behaviour must be your primary value (at least as far as anyone else is concerned). If you say that your health is your primary value but do not support this by your behaviour, then either you are seriously misleading yourself or you need to change your behaviour.

Remember the example of Tom (the manager who abandoned time management)? Tom spent most of his energy at work although he would have claimed that his family was his primary value. He would arrive home and slump in a chair, often still thinking about work. He had little remaining energy for his family.

Be prepared to give priority to different values at different times

Tom could have done this but instead he became overwhelmed by his work. One of his values got all his energy, while the other had none. Had Tom stated clearly when each of these values had priority he might have reconciled these two important parts of his life. He might have explained to his family and his colleagues that while work would be his priority at the office and maybe for two evenings a week, his family would be his priority the rest of the time. This would mean, for example, that weekend work would become the exception rather than the rule.

Give quality time

Giving energy is not the same as giving time. In terms of actual hours spent, Tom gave a lot of time to his family, but he gave them very little of his energy. When we talk about giving someone or something some of our time, we need to think in terms of quality time – of time with energy.

A good example of this is the case of Paul. Paul had moved in, temporarily, with his girlfriend while his own house was being decorated. He was kept busy with his house and his work, attending social engagements with clients and colleagues. He still saw more of his girlfriend than he had done previously, although this was mainly late at night or early in the morning.

Paul soon realised that things were not working out as well as he had hoped. His girlfriend was not happy because although they spent more hours together, they had little quality time. The situation was made worse by the apparent quality time Paul spent elsewhere.

The solution was simple. They agreed to set aside one evening a week as their evening – their quality time together.

Summary

- Decide what your long-term goals are, and from time to time, reappraise them to see if you want to change direction. Check that your pattern of behaviour is moving you towards your goals.

- Set objectives at the outset for every important task; keep a 'To do' list of tasks to be done.

- Sort tasks into order of priority and, as a rule of thumb, do the most important tasks first.

- Set aside some uninterrupted Thinking Time when you can reflect on lessons to be learned from the past, anticipate problems in the future and set contingency plans to allow for likely possibilities.

- Plan time for life outside work – time for holidays and leisure activities and time to relax. You will then be more effective during the time you are at work.

Your points:

_____

_____

_____

_____

_____

_____

_____

Putting it into practice

1. Review a typical week (try to choose an actual week). What were two things that went wrong or two things you didn't get done? How might things have been improved if you had managed your time better?

2. Set objectives for three activities you will do this week. Write them out in your diary.

   Review your objectives one week later. Were they achieved? If not, why not?

3. Write a 'To do' list for your day (include what you want to get done outside work).

   Mark on your list which items are As, which Bs and which Cs.

   At the end of the day, see how effective you feel the list has been.

4. Think of all the under-used time you could turn into 'double time'. Select at least one period of time you will use this week and what you will use it for. For example:

   Waiting in a queue   Consciously relax
       at the bank   tense muscles

Personal Planner

Key points	Action to be taken

Further reading

Effective Time Management, Adair, J, 1988 (Pan)
A practical book with case studies of eminent people and organisations which outline their time management approaches. It contains practical exercises for self-development.

Managing Your Time, Seiwert, L J, 1989 (Kogan Page)
Another practical book which is very interactive and full of easy-to-use tips on time management.

CHAPTER 4

How to Communicate Effectively and Assertively with Others

In this chapter, you will learn:

- How to communicate effectively
- How to give a clear message
- How to back up your words
- How to put the ideas into action

Ineffective communication and stress

Poor and ineffective communication can place a lot of pressure on you and on the person or group with whom you are communicating. In recent research we have found that one of the key sources of pressure for individuals is not being clear about what is expected of them in their jobs.

When communication is not clear it is not effective. With unclear communication you can end up guessing what the other person wants (and you might guess incorrectly) or you can end up being angry, disappointed or even secretly triumphant because the other person hasn't guessed what it is you want. This all adds to the pressure of the job. All sorts of ends may be achieved by hidden and unclear messages, but effective communication will not be one of them.

What is effective communication?

In effective communication, each party knows what the others are saying and what their feelings are on the subject. Effective communication is open, direct and equal communication in which you know and state clearly what you want to take from or give to the situation and in which you can also identify what messages are being sent by the other participants. Your role as an effective communicator is twofold:

(a) you have to be clear about the message you want to send, and
(b) you have to be clear about the messages being sent by the other party.

What is assertive behaviour?

Assertive behaviour is fundamental to effective communication. Being assertive means:

1. Having certain qualities: self-confidence, self-respect;
2. Behaving in certain ways; acting in a rational and adult way, stating directly what you want;
3. Having a particular approach to life:
   - being honest
   - being positive
   - being straightforward;
4. Above all, treating others with the same respect and understanding that you expect for yourself.

How assertive behaviour assists effective communication

Assertive behaviour aids communication because it is based on the acknowledgement that all of us have certain fundamental rights. Assertiveness (and hence more effective communication) begins by accepting these rights and observing them in the way you behave.

Rights we all have

1. The right to ask for what we want or don't want.
2. The right to be listened to and respected.
3. The right not to know about something and not to understand.
4. The right to make mistakes.
5. The right to change our minds.

Do you accept your basic rights in the way you behave? Do you acknowledge the basic rights of others?

If these rights are new to you, try to put just one of them into practice for yourself and for others over the coming week. Then for each week that follows, note down a right you will observe. Watch how your behaviour changes and how others change in the way they interact with you.

Ten ground rules for assertive behaviour and effective communication

The following set of rules is general and comprehensive. You will not need to apply them all in every situation, nor will they have the same order of importance in all cases. Because of this, the rules are given in a fairly arbitrary order. The rest of this section shows how you can put assertiveness into practice in specific situations.

1. Be clear about what you want

Think out beforehand what it is you really want. For example, do you really want a perfect letter to go out to your customer or do you want to be angry with the typist because she/he is spending a lot of time talking to friends and not putting effort into the work? Or do you want both, and if so, which is the most important?

2. Make a clear statement

Make a statement and if necessary rehearse it.

3. Be calm and rational

Once you become heated it is easy to lose track of what the message is. Also, remember to put the emphasis on communication not on winning.

4. Be specific

Identify specifically and simply what you want, whether it is what you want the other to clarify or what you want to convey.

5. State your limitations and alternatives

Say clearly what you will do and what alternatives are available for those things you can't do.

6. Express what you feel

If the statement, request or response makes you happy, afraid or angry, say so. But say it clearly and then return to your point.

7. Do not be side-tracked

Listen to what is being said and then repeat your request, point, refusal or whatever. This is often called the 'broken record' technique.

8. Choose your time and place

Whenever possible, choose the most appropriate place to communicate and choose a time when the other person can listen. If you are caught at a time when you are unable to give your full attention, say so and delay the discussion (even if only for a few seconds) until you can attend fully.

9. Give reasons, not excuses

It is better to give reasons for what you want or do not want to do.

10. Be prepared to compromise or stand down from your 'need'

When you have stated clearly what you would like as the outcome and you have expressed your feelings if you need to, be prepared to accept the best solution for the situation. We are talking about effective communication, not how to win.

Six assertiveness tips

1. Take responsibility for what you say

In your choice of words remember that you are saying what you want or don't want when you are being assertive. You are giving a plain message: 'I know what I want and this is what it is.' You must therefore use 'I' (or 'My') and words that indicate you have chosen the action (eg prefer, choose, will, will not).

'Can't' or 'shouldn't are passive words. They show that you are not in control. They can even indicate that you might really want to do something other than what you are suggesting.

The other person can come up with arguments to counteract your 'can'ts' or 'shouldn'ts' but no one can argue with what you want to do.

Script

Use: 'I', 'My'	'Not: 'She/he says' 'They say'
Use: 'Will', 'Choose' 'Prefer', 'Will not'	Not: 'Can't 'Shouldn't'

---

2. Repeat what the other person says or requests before you respond

This shows that you understand the message and perhaps their feelings as well. It also helps you to check that they are asking exactly what you think they are asking. You can then respond. Remember that understanding what the other person wants does not mean you have to agree, but it can make it easier for them to accept your response.

> *Script*
>
> 'So what you are asking is . . .'
>
> 'You would like me to . . .'

3. Be prepared to ask for more details

It is often unreasonable to turn down a request you do not know enough about, or to react to what appears an unreasonable, perhaps sweeping, statement. Asking the person to explain a point in more detail, maybe to give an example of what they mean, can help to avoid unnecessary conflict. The person might not have meant exactly what you thought or perhaps had good reasons for saying what they said.

> *Script*
>
> 'Could you give me an example of what you mean?'
>
> 'I don't want to accept or reject this idea without all the data: I would like to know . . .'

4. Acknowledge the other person's feelings

Again, this demonstrates that you understand the situation and empathise with the other person, but that your decision will still be your own. Showing that you understand how they feel can help short-circuit any emotional blackmail they may be tempted to use.

> *Script*
>
> 'I know you have been hoping that I will take the new position and if I don't you will have to start again, but I have decided to stay put.'

5. Tell the other person how you feel and what you are going to do

Let the other person know the effect he or she is having and what you are going to do. This helps to avoid any surprises in a communication and ensures that the other person has to face up to your feelings as well as your actions.

Script

'I feel very strongly about this – I will not change my mind.'

'I feel quite taken aback by what you have just said. I would like to take five minutes to compose myself and think about it, then I will get back to you.'

'If you carry on in that way I will put the phone down.'

NB. Always be honest in what you say you will do, because you may have to follow it through. For example, if you say you will put the phone down, then be prepared to do so.

6. Don't apologise unless there is good reason

Do not apologise for what you do or say 'Sorry' merely because the other person is unlikely to be pleased. If you choose to do what you do, apologies will rarely be needed.

Unnecessary apologies compromise your position. If you want to compromise, it is far better to tackle it assertively, by saying, for example, 'I would like to find some middle ground.' This keeps you in charge of the situation and ensures that the communication is still open and honest, not locked in subtle games and hidden meanings.

Apologies are for when you have said or done something you regret: a simple and sincere 'Sorry' is usually enough. (Sometimes it can be good for your ego to add 'I was wrong'.) The matter is then closed.

Sometimes you will find that a person does not accept your

apology and still feels hard done by. Your conscience will tell you if your apology was enough. If you want to do more, try asking if there is anything you can do to help or, even better, suggest a concrete and specific action you are prepared to take. The onus is then on the other person to respond.

Script

Try: 'David, I've decided to give the job to Paul. I know you will be really disappointed. I will be happy to go over my reasons for the decision later, if you want.'

Not: 'David, I'm sorry, I've given the job to Paul. I know it's a pain but there's really nothing I can do. I would have liked to give you a chance but you can't please everyone. Sorry, but that's life.'

How to use assertiveness

You now have the ground rules for assertiveness and six tips to help you become a more assertive (and effective) communicator. But you may still be unhappy with your communication in specific areas. Here we have targeted five common difficulties you may encounter and identified ways of handling them effectively.

How to say 'No'

When you are refusing a request, try sticking to one theme and repeating it: stick to one set of words and repeat them. For example, saying 'No' again in the same words you used before emphasises that you are not going to change your mind. If, however, you give a new reason or a more drawn-out explanation, the other person can begin to attack this. The other person may try to beat down your reasons or just be persistent because you appear to be unsure.

In fact, you don't even need a reason to refuse a request – not wanting to do it is reason enough. You may choose to give a brief explanation out of politeness (eg, 'No I won't stay because I've arranged to see someone tonight') but this is not up for discussion. The key part of the message is 'No'. When you repeat yourself, try just saying 'No' without the explanation.

If you doubt the effectiveness of this, try it out with a friend. One of you ask the other for a favour (for example, 'Will you take my place at the meeting on Friday?' or 'May I borrow your room for an interview tomorrow?'). Try not to be put off. The person being asked should respond with a clear 'No' statement and repeat it.

Script

First request:	May I use your office this afternoon?
You:	No. I'll be using it myself.
Second request:	Go on, it's really important for me . . .
You:	No. I'll be using it myself.
Third request:	Look, it's just this once. Please.
You:	No.

Obviously, *how* you say 'No' is as important as what you say. If you say it firmly and clearly, even if you feel uncertain inside, your message will be effective.

You can also use eye contact to underline that the matter is closed. Look at the other person as you say 'No', then turn away – the conversation is finished.

Finally, bring together as many of the assertiveness tips as you can. This will apply to any communication, but in terms of saying 'No', you might do the following:

- Repeat the same words.
- Use 'I' to indicate that it is a personal choice – not a matter of 'can't' or 'shouldn't'.
- Let the other person know how you feel and what you will do ('I feel strongly about this – I will not change my mind').
- Don't apologise for your decision – stand by it.

- Look away when you have finished, to signal that the conversation is at an end.

How to avoid interruptions

Try to speak at a reasonably consistent speed. You will probably need to slow down your speech a little to do this – if you talk quickly you can end up talking in bursts and leaving gaps during which you can easily be interrupted.

Avoid eye contact with the person who is trying to interrupt you. Unless they can catch your eye, they will find it very difficult to interrupt. If the interrupter is persistent, stop for a moment and address him or her directly. Be prepared to say clearly how you feel, what you would like to happen and/or what you will do. Then turn straight back to the others and away from the interrupter.

Script

'I haven't quite finished.'

'I feel this point is too important to be left unsaid.'

'I would like to finish this point first.'

'Will you please wait a moment?'

How to gain a response

As you finish what you want to say, look directly at the person you want to respond. Hold the person's gaze and the silence.

Imagine you have been given an unacceptable room in an hotel. Rather than a drawn-out argument, try stating the situation simply and finishing with what you want (for example, 'I want another room'). Then *wait*.

The silence will encourage the other person to respond. You may have to be disciplined in this because silences can be awkward and we often like to qualify further what we have said. The silence will set off your request by way of contrast.

How to show you are listening

You may rate yourself a good listener – you may follow well what other people say – but do you show you are listening? Good listeners do this and it works to their benefit. If you are not a good social talker then at least try to be a good listener, for good listeners are often seen as good conversationalists. Try it out yourself. Put into practice the 'active listening' ideas below and see how many people turn to you afterwards and say, 'You've been really interesting to talk to.'

When you see your role as listener as an active rather than a passive one you will find you become more involved in a conversation. You will also understand much more because you will check what has been said.

Active listening tips: could you do any of the following more often?

- Confirm your understanding ('So, as I understand it, by saying X you also imply Y').
- Summarise key points ('The gist of your argument, then, is . . .').
- Ask for clarification ('What exactly do you mean by . . . ?').
- Refer back to something the talker said earlier ('You mentioned at the outset . . . How does that fit in?).
- Nod your head to show understanding.
- Use 'uh-huh' and other encouraging noises.
- Allow silences to extend before breaking in.

'Accustom yourself to give careful attention to what others are saying, and try your best to enter into the mind of the speaker.'

Marcus Aurelius, philosopher and Roman emperor

How to accept and give compliments

Giving and receiving compliments is almost a lost art in Britain, receiving compliments especially so. We often seem unable to accept a compliment unless we qualify it first. Imagine, for example, that someone says 'Well done' to you, for whatever reason. How would you respond? Would you qualify the praise, perhaps saying something similar to the sentences below?

Ways of qualifying praise

- Oh, I was a bit lucky with that one.
- You should have seen how I handled the same thing last week – it was a real disaster.
- Thanks – but it wasn't just me, we all did something.
- Thanks – but anyone could have done it.
- Oh, it was nothing.

Or could you accept the praise at full value?

Ways of accepting praise

- Say 'Thank you' and nothing more.
- Say 'Thank you' and agree with the praise (eg, 'I thought it went well too').
- Say 'Thank you' and return the compliment (eg, 'It is good of you to say so').
- Say 'Thank you' and say why you agree (eg, 'I thought a stand-up presentation would communicate the facts better than a written report').

When you give a compliment, be clear and precise about what you are saying. For example, 'I liked the way you kept control of that meeting.'

If you want to make a general point, try to make it real by giving a couple of specific examples. Saying, 'Your great strength is your interpersonal skills' does not, alone, say much to anyone. If you add 'for example, you handled old Mr Thomas very tactfully and you are very popular with your staff', the compliment is both clearer and more immediate.

Two more points about giving compliments: give them as soon as possible after the event (the longer you wait, the less impact the compliment will have) and, unlike criticism, give compliments in front of others. A shy person, complimented in private, may never share this news with colleagues. Praise given when there is an audience, on the other hand, makes that person a success to themselves and to others. Their feeling of self-esteem will rise much higher with the recognition of their contemporaries.

Useful tips for compliments

- Give more compliments.
- Be clear and precise.
- Give an example or examples.
- Compliment someone as soon after the event as possible.
- Give compliments in front of an audience.

It is not (just) what you say, it's the way that you say it

Whenever you make a statement, ask a question, make a request or use spoken communication for any of its many functions, the verbal content of what you say is only one part of the message. Other very important aspects are the non-verbal aspects: the voice, the inflection of the voice and the body language. When all these are giving the same message, your message has a good chance of being 100 per cent clear and effective to the listener. When there is a mismatch between them, the impact of what you say is very much reduced by the way that you say it.

If your verbal language is not clear, that is if you speak in English to someone who only speaks Greek, it is unlikely that you will be clearly understood. However, with signs and gestures, smiles and nods, some things can be communicated. What is not so immediately obvious is that if your verbal message is quite clear (that is, you have noted and used all the ground rules) and you then use inappropriate non-verbal language, your verbal language will be heard but not believed. If, for example, you say, 'I can manage perfectly well, thank you' in a whining voice as you struggle to hold open a door with your foot and manoeuvre a chair through it, you are less likely to be believed than when you give the same message in a clear, firm voice having wedged the door open first. It has been demonstrated many times that when there is a difference between the verbal and the non-verbal content of a message, the non-verbal is likely to be believed.

So what can you do about it? Remember that we are still talking about situations where you want to be effective and assertive.

Be sincere

Don't give ambiguous messages. This way it is more likely that your body language will be congruent with your spoken message.

Be aware of the range of your voice

'Speak slowly and audibly while delivering a message' is perhaps the most obvious piece of information that can be offered about clear and effective communication. Although it is obvious, actually doing this when you are offering criticism or repeating a request isn't always easy. Practise using the full range of your voice, be aware of how it feels when you are speaking quickly, speaking slowly. Relaxing the neck, throat and chest helps you to breathe more deeply and project your voice more fully.

Be aware of the inflections in your voice

Changes in inflection, pitch and tone can convey different messages. If you are making an assertive statement, don't let your voice rise at the end of the sentence and make it sound like a question. An 'edge' to your voice can make a refusal sound like a put-down and an assertive statement sound aggressive. If there is ambiguity in what you say and the way that you are saying it, remember that other people are likely to respond to the tone of your voice rather than the content of your message. Keeping a steady and calm voice can only be done in conditions in which you feel calm and steady or where you have a great deal of awareness and self-monitoring. So, if you want to remain calm and you feel that anger or self-pity are beginning to affect your thoughts, take a deep breath and very carefully and deliberately (not with exasperation) speak in an even tone. Reminding yourself that you wish to be assertive can help you keep your voice calm and conversely keeping your voice calm can help you to be assertive.

If you communicate a lot on the telephone, then having an 'assertive' voice and a clear message will go a long way towards ensuring effective communication. But most of our communication is carried out face to face and therefore the additional dimension of body language needs to be monitored. Popular magazines often tell us about one specific gesture, for example, 'scratching the nose means the scratcher is telling a lie' . . . or maybe his nose itches! Single gestures are like single words – they have some meaning. But in a cluster, like words in a sentence, they carry a clearer message. Set in a context, they are clearer still.

Posture

The way in which you hold yourself says a lot about you. Hunching your shoulders upwards towards your ears is a gesture that often accompanies anxiety. Therefore, if you generally stand or sit like this you may be seen as anxious. Likewise, sitting with your arms folded can indicate a defensive feeling and sitting with your hands on your head a feeling of superiority.

The unfortunate thing is that posture is often the result of habit and can convey false information about how you are feeling. It is therefore doubly important when you are being assertive, that you convey an appropriate message through your posture.

If you have a real problem and feel very uncomfortable with a different posture, there are at least two solutions. One is to compensate for the false message by all the other messages that you convey. The second concerns only those who do wish to change, and that is to enrol with a teacher of the Alexander Technique and learn the art of good body alignment. (See the list of Further Reading on page 84 for information on the Alexander Technique.)

Relative height

Sitting or standing level with the person you are talking to gives the feeling of equality. Added height gives an indication of superiority and power (hence the hands-on-head gesture). If you are sitting lower down than the person you are talking to, stand up or perch on the desk. Do all you can to make your heights equal.

Proximity and distance

We all have a distance from one another at which we feel comfortable. There is a cultural bias to this. It has been observed that people from hot 'Latin' countries need to be closer than most others, while 'Nordics' need a much greater distance. This personal space or 'bubble' is most important to us. If someone moves in too close we move away; if we are too distant we move in closer. It is only when we get it right that we can be comfortable, effective communicators. You have most effect when you approach and face someone squarely and at the most appropriate distance. This may involve moving right up to their desk, but do it before you begin to speak.

Eye contact

All the time we are talking to someone face to face we are looking for a reaction. Their eyes tell us whether they are listening or not, whether they are involved in what we are saying or whether they are intrigued, intimidated or just plain bored. It is impossible to communicate with someone who is looking at a television or a visual display unit or if they have their back to you. It is also very difficult to talk to someone who stares all the time and never breaks their gaze. Effective communication depends on being able to engage and hold the other's eyes but to vary that gaze to the rest of the face as you talk.

If all this seems impossible and too much to change, don't worry. The reason that the voice and body are so effective in communication is because people use them this way without thinking. It is the naturalness with which they are used which makes them believable and dependable aspects of communication. When what you say and what you mean are in accord, there is no problem. You don't have to think about what you are doing, it just happens.

You need only to be careful, when you want to subdue your reactions and feelings, to keep the communication effective and your behaviour assertive. Getting the message right on these occasions means not only getting the words right but conveying the same message with your body and your voice.

Summary

- Remember that the fundamental aim of communication is to be clear about the message you want to send and the message being sent to you. Any strategies you use are just ways of achieving this clarity.

- Respect your assertiveness rights and the assertiveness rights of others in the way you behave.

- Use the ten ground rules and the six assertiveness tips to guide your behaviour.

- Consider how your communication will be received by others – what messages are you sending? Remember that verbal communication carries only part of the message: keep your non-verbal behaviour consistent with the verbal content of your message.

Your points:

_____

_____

_____

_____

_____

_____

_____

_____

Putting it into practice

1. Practise giving clear messages in 'easy' situations, and ask for what you really want rather than give a subtle message. For example, 'Could you open the window, please?' instead of 'How can you work in this heat?'

2. Monitor your own behaviour for a few minutes each day. During those few minutes, make every statement or query effective.

3. At the end of the day, list those situations where you wish you had been more effective. Stop if your list goes beyond three. Mentally go back over those situations and decide what would be the effective way to have handled them. Ask yourself, 'What was it I wanted to get from that situation?'

   Select the easiest of the three and rehearse the way in which you will handle it effectively in future.

4. List your top five points from this section. Rather than trying to implement all of these at once, try to keep to one of the points each week for the next few weeks. Note down a review date in your diary.

Personal Planner

Key points	Action to be taken

Further reading

General texts

A Woman in Your Own Right, Dickson, A, 1982 (Quartet Books)
A comprehensive book about general assertiveness. Particularly aimed at women, but most of the ideas are applicable to both sexes.

A good book if you like a framework to help you to understand things. The book is based on an approach called 'Transactional Analysis'. You need not become a convert of this approach to gain some useful insights.

How to Win Friends and Influence People, Carnegie, D, 1981 (Cedar Books)
Basic principles for dealing with others. You may be surprised how many basic principles are neglected.

Specific texts

Assert Yourself: How to Reprogramme Your Mind for Positive Action, Lindenfield, G, 1987 (Thorsons)
An easy-to-read 'do-it-yourself' book on assertiveness. It is full of practical tips and includes exercises on assertiveness for both groups and individuals.

Assertiveness at Work, Back, K and Back, K, 1982 (McGraw-Hill)
A guide to recognising and practising different levels of assertiveness in the work situation.

CHAPTER 5

How to Relax Before, During and After the Event

In this chapter, you will learn:

- How to relax quickly in the middle of the working day
- How to relax deeply
- How to release pent-up emotion safely
- How to make the most of sleep

Practical ways to relax

Before you read on, a distinction must be made between the terms 'relaxing' and 'relaxation'. Relaxation is used when referring to deep muscular relaxation; relaxing is used to refer to quick and easy ways of easing tension.

How can a busy person relax?

There is a lot of nonsense spoken and written about relaxing. This is probably why it is so sadly under-used by people at work. One belief is that 'relaxing takes a long time'. How often have you heard someone say, 'I don't have time to relax'? Another belief is that relaxing means deep meditation and hard-to-follow techniques. Yet another belief is that relaxing is something we do afterwards, to wind down. Many people's idea of relaxing is a long hot bath *after* a hard and tiring day.

These beliefs are misleading: there are quick ways to relax; there are simple ways to relax. These quick and simple ways to relax make relaxing possible *throughout* the working day and not just last thing at night.

You will understand this better if we compare relaxing with eating out. Sometimes you will choose a fast-food meal for convenience. At other times you will eat a four-course meal – you choose whatever is appropriate to the moment. It is the same with relaxing.

What is relaxing?

Relaxing is just winding down. It is as simple as that. In this way, we are like the old mechanical toys which had keys in their backs to wind them up. Our keys are wound up by stress; we unwind by relaxing. The comparison goes further. Like the toys, we need some dynamic tension to operate. But if you wind us up too far, we reach breaking point. We are different from toys in at least one critical respect: we can stop the build-up of tension and unwind whenever we choose.

When to relax

Relax *before* any potentially stressful event

You enter each new situation carrying some residual tension. The next stressful event will add to that tension. If you know that the next event may be stressful, do a quick self-check. Ask yourself, 'How stressed am I now?' If you feel fairly wound up before the event, how are you going to perform during it?

Stop for a moment to wind down. Close your eyes and take a few deep breaths *before* you knock on the MD's door. You do not need to wind down completely. Just unwind your 'key' a few turns to allow yourself the capacity to tackle the business in hand.

Relax *during* stressful events

Stress does not wait for the most convenient time to emerge. When are you most likely to feel stressed? It is right in the middle of a stressful event; when you are in front of the MD; or giving a presentation to a client; or handling any crisis situation.

This is precisely when you least want to lose control. You need to calm down quickly and stay calm. You want to activate ways of relaxing *now*, not wait until afterwards.

Relax *after* stressful events

Each stressful event follows hot on the heels of the last. The danger here is that the stress of several minor events can accumulate to become a major problem. Regular deep relaxation allows you to wind down completely and be better prepared for whatever lies ahead.

How to work *and* relax

Here are 14 tips for everyday relaxing:

1. Slow down your breathing

Take a few deep breaths and exhale slowly each time. Try this before you knock on the MD's door, or even in the middle of a stressful presentation.

Controlled breathing is one of the easiest ways to calm down quickly. It helps because it counteracts part of the stress response. When we are stressed, breathing becomes shallower and more erratic. In extreme circumstances you may even gasp for breath. This can quite quickly lead to panic or a feeling of being out of control. Fortunately, a few deep breaths can reverse the process. Some people also find it helps to imagine the tension slipping away as the breath is exhaled.

2. Use exercise to wind down

Physical activity releases the energy and the muscle tension built up by stress. This is why a game of squash can feel so good after a hard day at work.

So when is it best to exercise? Whenever you feel stress build up, work out how you can release it. If you feel stressed before a meeting, for example, go for a short walk to release that nervous tension. If you have had a frustrating morning, arrange to do some physical activity during lunch-time so that you can return, relaxed, in the afternoon.

Try to do some physical activity on a regular basis. Paul Mathews, former Assistant Director of Engineering at British Gas South East, told us that this is what he does. He tries to keep to a motto of 'Take it when you can get it'. In other words, he aims to take advantage of any opportunity for physical activity. After travelling on the tube, for example, he might walk up the stairs rather than using the escalator.

Such 'everyday' physical activity helps to prevent the accumulation of stress (see Chapter 6 on page 85 for more information on the use of exercise to manage stress).

3. Relax your muscles directly

The stress response produces muscular tension, so the aches and pains that you feel are not imaginary. Concentrate on where your body feels tense. Likely areas where tension often accumulates include the back, the neck and shoulders and the stomach. However, don't confine yourself to these areas. Find out where you feel stressed. Drivers, for example, often find their facial muscles tense as they concentrate on the road.

When you know where the tension is, let that part of your body relax. Just let go. Feel the tension ease away.

One way to help the muscles to relax is to tense them first. Muscles relax more deeply after being tensed. Clench your fist tightly, then let it unclench and you will feel how this works. So, stretch or tense the aching muscles, then let them go. Repeat this a couple of times for maximum benefit. Neck muscles can be relaxed by gently rolling your head around in a circular motion, first one way then the other (see 'Deeper Relaxation' on page 73).

For deeper muscular relaxation, invest in a thorough massage, or learn to do massage at home with a partner. Basic massage is easy to do and very relaxing. A couple of good books are introduced in the list of Further Reading on page 84.

4. Check the way you sit and stand

Muscle tension can be exacerbated by bad posture. The two simplest things you can do about this are to check the way you sit and the way you stand and walk. The golden rule for both is to keep your spine as straight as possible. The Alexander Technique has been developed to help people correct their posture (for more information, see the list of Further Reading on page 84).

Change your work area if you have to stretch or sit at uncomfortable angles for long periods. See if your firm will invest in an ergonomically sound chair.

Make a conscious effort to avoid slumped shoulders. You will feel better for it. If the problem persists it might be worth checking how you sleep. A firm mattress is better for you than a soft one. Once you are used to it you will probably sleep better too.

5. Release tension emotionally

Physical activity can be useful in releasing tension. Physiologically it helps to use up the adrenalin created by the stress in the situation. When physical activity is not possible you can still work out a lot of tension just sitting at your desk. We generate tension just by holding in what we feel. We can't yell at the MD. We can't be rude to a customer. And we can't alway say what we want to some of our colleagues.

One way of releasing these frustrating pent-up emotions is to write them down. Write the kind of letter or memo you would really like to send to someone who has annoyed you. List every grievance you can think of and when you are satisfied that the letter properly represents your views, put it to one side. Come back to it tomorrow. Then, if you still feel infuriated by the points you wrote down, you may have to think about how to tackle them positively. If your tension really was just a reaction of the moment, you can throw away the letter – and you haven't made a fool of yourself or offended others.

If you have a dictaphone, you can record your thoughts on tape. Listening to them later, you will probably be able to tell which of them are motivated by emotion rather than reason. (Make sure you store these tapes and/or letters in a secure place.)

'Writing is a form of therapy'

Graham Greene

6. Release tension by talking to a friend

If you do not want to record your feelings, why not discuss them with a friend? For some people, putting feelings into words is the easiest way to release pent-up emotions and it is one reason why the army has debriefing sessions. It provides an opportunity to 'talk yourself down' from a stressful experience. Sometimes the other person can talk you down but more often the onus is on you; the other person is just an ear. There is more than a little truth in the idea that 'Just talking helps'.

If you arrange a debriefing, set the ground rules in advance. This can prevent the session from degenerating into pointless argument. Good ground rules allow you to say whatever you feel, however unreasonable it may seem. There is no need to rationalise the problem or justify action. The purpose is for you to 'get it off your chest'. The result should be that you have 'cooled off' and unwound ready for the next task ahead of you.

If you do not regularly let go of at least some of your stress, you run the danger of allowing it to build up. This can produce what psychologists call the upward spiral of tension and downward spiral in performance.

7. Slow down physically

When we rush around non-stop all day long we heighten the feeling of being stressed. Of course, sometimes the nature of the work will mean that you have to operate at high speed; but it is when you are operating like this that you can suddenly reach your breaking point.

One solution, if you really cannot afford a break, is to slow down for a while in order to 'catch up with yourself'. A teacher did this when faced with a troublesome class. Normally he would rush from class to class. About to teach a troublesome class, however, he would walk slowly and deliberately between classrooms. He explained that he had no time to take a break between classes. Walking slowly helped him to calm down mentally and select the right frame of mind for the job ahead.

Are there times when you could slow down? How about limiting yourself to 70 mph on the motorway? Or walking slowly – not rushing – from your office to the meeting room. You will find your performance is better afterwards.

8. Take a break

A 'go-slow' period is a short-term emergency measure. In the long term, it is no substitute for taking a break. Yet there are many people in business who seem to think it 'macho' to work through without taking breaks.

These people are doing themselves and their organisations a disservice. Breaks improve performance; the longer you go without a break, the further your performance deteriorates. If you simply cannot fit in breaks because of your work, you may need to look at your time management.

The short message is that not taking breaks in order to save time is a false economy. The army rarely marches soldiers continually – it allows them to rest for a few minutes in every hour. In this way they will march further, more quickly. FW Taylor, who wrote *The Principles of Scientific Management*, applied this rule to business. Merely by instructing a labourer to rest when he was told, Taylor improved the man's performance almost fourfold. From loading 12.5 tons of pig iron per day he was able to load 47 tons per day, and he still was not exhausted. This performance was no freak peak. During the next three years, the labourer continued to maintain this standard.

The golden rule of breaks is, 'Take a break *before* you feel tired.' Soldiers can march for longer than an hour before needing a break. Taylor's labourer was instructed to rest even though he was not tired. Try this yourself and see how much more you accomplish in a day.

It does not matter if your breaks are short. If you take regular breaks, you will not need so long anyway. It is far better to have frequent 'breathers' than one long rest in the middle of the day (although this can vary a little from person to person).

9. Have a change of activity

Quality is just as important as quantity. How you use your break will determine how useful it is. Try to do something different from whatever you do the rest of the time. If you are indoors, sitting down all day, go for a walk or do some more vigorous exercise. If your work involves constantly dealing with others, award yourself some time alone. Remember the old saying, 'A change is as good as a rest'.

10. Take micro-breaks

What can you do when time really is pressing and you cannot afford even a 10- or 15-minute break? One technique to try is a 'micro-break'.

A micro-break lasts anything between 10 and 60 seconds. Less than 10 seconds and it is questionable whether you are really breaking off from work at all; and once you start measuring your breaks in minutes rather than seconds, they are not really micro-breaks any more.

Use micro-breaks to force a halt in the heat of the moment. Stop yourself for a few seconds when you feel yourself responding out of emotion rather than reason. This way you will appear more professional. You will offend fewer people, and you will make fewer regrettable, 'knee-jerk' decisions.

Making the most of a micro-break

Shut out any external distractions. Close your eyes if it helps to do this.

Shut off thoughts about the issue in hand. Concentrate instead on neutral thoughts – like counting down the seconds, or focusing on things your senses can detect which you miss in the usual hustle and bustle of the day: the ticking of the clock; your breathing; the smells in the air.

Whether you are sitting down or standing, try to keep your spine straight (this reduces tension throughout your body and aids relaxing). Let your muscles relax: allow arms and legs to 'flop'. Work through your body, identifying areas which are tense and then relaxing the muscles.

Breathe in more deeply and slowly exhale.

Pause for a moment before returning to your work. Reassess what needs to be done and what you must do first.

---

11. Take time to think

Don't just jump straight back into the fray after your micro-break. This defeats its purpose. Pause for a moment. Reassess what it is you are about to tackle. What needs to be done? What should you do first?

12. Set up escape mechanisms for yourself

These are ways of calling a halt when you feel the pressure begin to mount. The further you go, the faster the pressure mounts: it is like being caught in an upward spiral.

One way to insure against this upward spiral of pressure (and its associated downward spiral in performance) is to build in escape mechanisms. These are previously agreed actions to be taken if the situation becomes so stressful that continuing would be unproductive.

You can agree such actions with yourself, for example, 'If I find I begin to have a headache I will stop and take a short walk.'

Or you can set agreements with others, such as, 'If either of us feels we are becoming too emotional we can call a halt and reconvene later.'

13. Give yourself quiet times alone

Do not underestimate the value of time to yourself. We often become fraught merely because we are bombarded with so much going on around us. Quiet times allow us to relax without resorting to deeper relaxation techniques.

Try allotting yourself half an hour's quiet time at the end of the day. Some people find it helpful to sit in their car for ten minutes before leaving the car park. They wait until the 'rush' for the exit is over and then leave in a more relaxed frame of mind.

One full-time teacher, who is also a wife, mother and voluntary counsellor, takes her quiet time when she gets in from school. Her signal to her family is the newspaper. Whenever she is behind the newspaper it is 'Do not disturb' time. In fact, she says, she never reads a word but shuts off and refreshes herself before launching into another period of activity.

If you have a partner, agree on quiet times with each other. You should see the benefit almost immediately.

Once you are used to quiet times, see if you can use them at work.

How to give yourself time off work

- Micro-breaks: 10–60 seconds' calming down time whenever you need it.
- Regular breaks: schedule a few minutes every hour or so. Take a break *before* you feel tired.
- Standard breaks: you should be given lunch, tea and coffee breaks as standard. Use them.
- Quiet times: time to yourself, in the middle of a hectic day if possible; certainly at the end of the day.
- Holidays: they are there for a reason. You will be more effective if you take them.

---

14. Develop your release mechanism

Release mechanisms are the triggers which help you to relax. Listening to music, reading and walking are popular release mechanisms. Find out what works for you and build it into your regular routine. Just as dentists recommend regular brushing to prevent plaque and delay tooth decay, so psychologists recommend regular relaxing to control the growth and harmful effects of stress.

'The most important thing to me is listening to music – I do that most evenings.'

Jeffrey Bernard, *Spectator* and *Mirror* columnist

Make the most of your sleep

Stress often leads to sleep problems and poor sleep means you won't 'recharge your batteries' fully, making you more vulnerable to stress the next day. Fortunately, there are numerous tactics

71

you can try to help you to get the sleep you need. Here is a selection:

- Establish a routine of retiring (and rising) at regular times. This helps your body adjust to a certain rhythm.

- Take some physical exercise earlier in the evening so that your body really needs the rest.

- Take a short walk before going to bed.

- Begin to wind down an hour or so before retiring.

- Don't eat a heavy meal too soon before retiring. (A small snack is all right.)

- Have a milk drink (preferably a hot one) just before you retire. The calcium will help you to rest.

- Have a relaxing bath before retiring.

- If you have something on your mind, talk it through or mentally rehearse how you will handle it. Go to bed when you are satisfied that you have worked through the problem.

- Put your thoughts and worries literally on one side by writing them down before you retire. You can review them in the morning.

- Keep a pen and paper by your bedside. If you are troubled by thoughts in the night or struck by a great idea, you can dash it down and return to sleep.

- Close your eyes and think of sleeping. Picture the word 'yawn'. Imagine what it feels like to yawn and to feel sleepy.

- If you wake up, do not stay in bed. Get up and do something. When you feel tired, go back to bed. (You should not need to keep up this behaviour for more than a few nights at most.)

Deeper relaxation

What is relaxation?

Is relaxation going dancing, dining out, watching or playing sport, gardening? These and a host of other activities are relaxing things to do and can be both therapeutic and enjoyable, even though the same activity will not be viewed in the same way by everyone. However, as well as doing things that are generally relaxing, you can practise specific, deeper relaxation techniques. Such techniques involve a deliberately practised skill which restores the body, calms the mind and counterbalances the effects of stress.

The techniques can be active or passive. Active relaxation involves the use of exercises for your body or your mind and results in deep, peaceful relaxation. Passive relaxation also results in the same deep, peaceful state but this time someone else does the work – you hand control over to them.

Active relaxation

This consists, first, of exercises which use the bodily movements to relax the muscles and this in turn relaxes the mind. The activities which do this are:

- Yoga
- Tension/relaxation exercises
- Progressive relaxation exercises

In addition, there are the activities which use the mind to relax the body. The activities which do this are:

- Meditation
- Visualisation
- Autogenic training
- Self-hypnosis
- Rhythmical breathing

Passive relaxation

This too can involve work on the body which in turn relaxes the mind. The activities concerned include:

- Gentle massage
- Reflexology
- Aromatherapy

Passive relaxation also includes work on the mind to relax the body. An example of this is hypnotherapy.

Ideal methods of relaxation for different situations

'The ideal place for relaxation is on a warm sunny beach with the sound of waves breaking on the shore nearby', or so we read the other day. Actually, this is fine for some people and an ideal place for practising relaxation skills, but for others, particularly the very active, very harassed Type A (or 'must hurry' type) person, the very idea would cause additional stress.

So we have to look at relaxation first in relation to the needs of the person practising the skill. For the Type A person, the tension/relaxation and the rhythmical breathing methods are the best. They will give him or her a feeling of control, fit into a short space of time, bring quick results and can be practised in an office.

For those people who feel they cannot 'make' themselves relax, a reflexology or aromatherapy session is a good beginning. However, eventually, if they are to enjoy and benefit from relaxation, they should begin to practise active methods and start to take control. It is here that the use of a relaxation tape would be of great benefit.

You can locate sources of information about organisations where you can find teachers of yoga, autogenic training, meditation and practitioners of reflexology and aromatherapy, so the main focus in this material will be on those methods of relaxation which are safe and effective to practise on your own – those where you can take control and where the opportunity to practise them can be built into your daily planning. The methods include:

- Progressive relaxation

- Neck and shoulder relaxation
- Even breathing

What relaxation does for your body

Practising relaxation has a physiological effect. Your heart rate slows, your breathing becomes slower, a number of hormones are released into your bloodstream which enhance the feeling of calmness, and the reduction of tension. This physiological effect takes place whether the process begins with the breathing, the muscle relaxation or the mental relaxation exercises. The important thing to note is that it is physiologically impossible for the body to be tense and relaxed at the same time. In addition, relaxation counterbalances the effects of the stress response at the physiological level.

How to begin: action planning for relaxation

Decide which method would be most comfortable for you:

- Active or passive
- Using your mind to relax your body or using your body to relax your mind.

Find the means to carry out your chosen method of relaxation:

- Buy a relaxation tape.
- Find out about local facilities, eg yoga classes.
- Find a registered hypnotherapist, a recommended reflex-ologist.

Choose a place and a time to practise relaxation:

- On your own at home, in your quiet time
- With your partner and/or family
- In the office alone at lunch-time (an open-plan office may be less than ideal)
- Form a relaxation group with your colleagues and practise at lunch-times
- In the car before you leave for home (breathing and relaxation exercises are ideal for this situation)

Plan your programme:

- Plan to practise your method of relaxation daily and weekly.
- Plan short and regular daily sessions (one yoga exercise, a self-administered neck or foot massage, relaxation of the neck, face and shoulders, five minutes' deep, rhythmical breathing).
- Plan a longer weekly session (a class, a visit to a therapist, a total body relaxation).

Incorporate relaxation into your time management

- Having planned your time, place and method, put this in your diary as you would any other activity.
- Plan a review of your progress after two weeks and again after one month.
- Ask yourself if the relaxation has improved your feeling of well-being. Do you need to do more, do you need to do less?

Points to remember

1. Relaxation is a self-control method, a skill which must be practised.
2. Begin with sessions of 20–30 minutes a day, and reduce as skill increases.
3. Don't fall asleep.
4. Early in relaxation training you may be overly aware of your physical functioning. Don't be alarmed by this and learn to control it.
5. Strange sensations are common, eg tingling.
6. The ability to concentrate varies from day to day, so don't be discouraged if you find sustained concentration difficult. Do not, however, allow yourself to mull over problems while attempting to relax.
7. If you have heart or back/neck problems, do not attempt relaxation exercises involving breathing techniques or manipulation of the shoulders/neck without first consulting your doctor.
8. Always come out of relaxation slowly. Take a few deep breaths, slowly stretch and move your head around. Count to 10 as you slowly and gradually come back to your working day.

Instructions for progressive relaxation

1. Choose a quiet, solitary setting and comfortable chair with head support.
2. Any time will do but working people usually find early evening fits in best. Do not attempt relaxation within one hour of bed-time, as you are likely to fall asleep.
3. Try not to move around once relaxation has begun, unless your position is uncomfortable.
4. Relaxation sequence:

    (a) Tighten each muscle group while breathing in.
    (b) Hold position and breath for about 7–8 seconds.

(c) Breathe out and release tension (quickly).
(d) Repeat for each of the following muscle groups:

> right fist, right upper arm (by pressing elbows back),
> left fist, left upper arm,
> raise eyebrows, wrinkle eyes and nose,
> clench teeth, pull mouth corners down and press tongue to roof of mouth,
> neck (by pressing back against chair), shoulders,
> stomach, thighs (by pressing down heels),
> right lower leg (toes curled down), right foot (toes curled up),
> left lower leg, left foot

5. During tensing, concentrate on feelings of strain and tautness. During relaxation, concentrate on feelings of warmth and heaviness.
6. Between each clench–release episode, remain quiet and motionless for 10–15 seconds. Concentrate on maintaining relaxation. Repeat 'relax' in your head.
7. After all muscle groups have been relaxed, remain seated for several minutes, concentrating on feelings of relaxation and heaviness. Breathe slowly, regularly.

Relaxation of the neck and shoulders

Imagine two strings coming down from the ceiling above you, each one connected to one of your shoulders so that your shoulders could be lifted by them. With your arms completely relaxed, raise both your shoulders as if pulled up by these two imaginary strings. Lift them as high as you can and hold them. Feel the pull of the large muscles across the shoulders. Now relax. Drop your shoulders as if the strings had been cut. Allow them to sag as far as they will. Let all these shoulder muscles relax. Experience the effortless, pleasant relaxation. Notice how the feelings of relaxation spread throughout your body. Relax the muscles in your scalp. Smooth out your forehead. Relax your eyes and all your facial muscles. Let your jaw sag comfortably.

Now tighten the muscles in your forehead and scalp by

wrinkling up your forehead and raising your eyebrows at the same time. Hold it. Now relax. Let your brow smooth out and relax completely.

Now tense your jaw muscles by biting your teeth together. Bite hard, noticing the feeling of tightness in your jaw muscles. Now relax. Let your jaws go completely limp. Feel the surge of relief as relaxation flows in.

Now push the tip of your tongue against the roof of your mouth, so you can feel tightness in the muscles under your chin and in front of your throat. Push hard. Hold it. Now relax. Feel the sensation of relaxation stream down the sides of your face, under your chin, and into your throat, your whole body becoming more and more totally relaxed. Again, relax all the muscles in your cheeks and jaws. Let your whole face become as totally relaxed as your arms and shoulders; thoroughly and deeply relaxed.

Now push your head back as far as it will go. Hold it. Observe the pressure in the back of your neck. Now relax. Let your head return to its normal position. Now bend your head forward, touching your chin to your chest. Feel the tightness in the back of your neck. Now relax. Return your head to its normal, comfortable position. Once again, go on relaxing calmly and peacefully.

Breathing techniques

Diaphragmatic breathing

Place one hand on your chest and the other hand on your stomach. As you breathe in (inhale) picture a balloon gently filling up in your stomach and pushing it out. As you breathe out (exhale) allow your stomach to relax. The hand on your chest should not be moving while the hand on your stomach should be going up and down. Do not force your breath.

Practice: Breathe this way for a few minutes upon wakening n the morning, before relaxing and before sleeping. Continue your practice until this *normal* method of breathing is re-established.

Benefit: Chest breathing keeps the body in an aroused state, while diaphragmatic breathing encourages a relaxed state. Chest breathing also forces the body to work harder to receive the same amount of oxygen as diaphragmatic breathing.

Even breathing

As you inhale, count how long it takes and count the same number as you exhale (ie, breathe in 1–2–3–4, breathe out 1–2–3–4). After you have established a fairly slow, even breathing rhythm, you may stop counting and focus on your breath flowing out evenly without any pauses or jerks, including the pause between in and out. As you are breathing in be aware also that you are breathing from the diaphragm.

When to use: For instant relaxation, in combination with other relaxation techniques or as a relaxation technique in itself.

Benefit: The jerkier the breath the more disruptive it is to the autonomic nervous system. Even breathing relaxes your system.

'Two-to-one' breathing

Count approximately twice as long when you exhale as when you inhale (ie, 3 in – 6 out, 4 in – 8 out, etc). Breathe out as long as is comfortable (not necessarily *exactly* twice as long). You are not trying to fill or empty your lungs totally. After you have established a comfortable rhythm you may stop counting and focus on smooth diaphragmatic breathing.

When to use

Use when you need to calm down quickly, when you are feeling especially anxious or as a lead in to other relaxation techniques. *Do not use* when you are feeling depressed (use *even breathing*).

Summary

- Identify and practise ways to relax *before, during* and *after* stressful events.

- Recognise that everyday relaxing doesn't have to take long or involve complex techniques. You only need to build things into your routine that take the pressure off for a while (like regular breaks, for example).

- Complement your everyday relaxing by finding your own method of deep relaxation. Once you have a method, choose a time and a place to practise your deep relaxation regularly.

- Don't accept disturbed sleep as inevitable when you are under pressure. There are numerous tactics you can use to help you sleep – find those that work for you. Remember that sleeping tablets are a short-term and unsatisfactory solution.

Your points:

_____

_____

_____

_____

_____

_____

_____

_____

Putting it into practice

1. List anything you currently do *before*, *during* and *after* stressful events to help you to relax. If you are not satisfied with your lists, add one new strategy to each list. Check your progress in putting these three ways of relaxing into practice over the next week.

2. Monitor your working routine for two days. Note down any breaks you take from work when you really get the chance to switch off. Note down any breaks where you have to compromise with work. Review your lists. If you find that you compromise in more than a couple of breaks, concentrate on what you can do to protect your break periods. (Try, for example, leaving the building, giving a clear message that you are unavailable and will be back at a specific time, delegating responsibility while you are on a break).

3. Find a friend or close colleague you can talk to when you want to let off steam. Ask this person if they would agree to your using them as a sounding board when you want to release tension by getting something off your chest. If they agree, set the ground rules carefully. You should be able to say what you want, in total confidence and without being judged – in other words, just let it all pour out for, say three to four minutes. Then, if you choose, you can review your feelings more objectively.

4. Choose a method of deep relaxation. Set aside the time and place to try it out three times. After the third time, review how useful you think the technique is for (a) yourself, and (b) others.

Personal Planner

Key points	Action to be taken

Further reading

The Alexander Technique, Hodgkinson, L, 1988 (Judy Piatkus)
  A useful book for those who wish to know more about the Alexander Technique and the benefits of correct posture. This is not a 'do-it-yourself' guide to the technique.

The Book of Stress Survival, Kirsta, A, 1986 (Guild)
  A very practical book which has a particularly good section on short- and long-term remedies for stress.

The Complete Book of Massage, Maxwell-Hudson, C, 1988 (Dorling Kindersley)

Massage Cures, Davies, N and Harrold, F, 1990 (Thorsons)
  Both this book and the above give an introduction to massage and explain the techniques with the aid of pictures and diagrams.

You Must Relax, Jacobsen, E, 1980 (Unwin)
  This book is a guide to stress and its prevention through relaxation. It gives practical advice on how to relax physically and mentally when resting or during activity.

CHAPTER 6

How to Keep Your Body Healthy and Fit to Cope with Stress

In this chapter, you will learn:

- How to spot the physical signs and symptoms of stress
- How to eat a healthy diet
- How to cut out unhealthy habits
- How to exercise for stamina, suppleness and health

Your body and stress

The physical stress response is merely the body gearing up for immediate action. The many physiological changes equip the body to respond instantly in the face of a threat.

Some of the key changes are shown in Figure 6.1.

What to look for

Watch out for signs of these physiological changes. These are the Early Warning Signals of stress. They include:

- Fast breathing (difficulty catching your breath)
- Dry mouth and throat
- Clammy palms
- Feeling hot
- Tense muscles
- Indigestion

You should not suffer from all of these all at once. But when you do experience them, remember that they are merely indicating everything else that is happening inside your body.

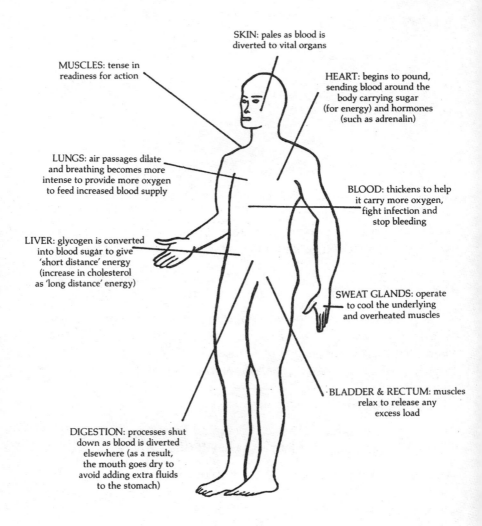

SKIN: pales as blood is diverted to vital organs

MUSCLES: tense in readiness for action

HEART: begins to pound, sending blood around the body carrying sugar (for energy) and hormones (such as adrenalin)

LUNGS: air passages dilate and breathing becomes more intense to provide more oxygen to feed increased blood supply

BLOOD: thickens to help it carry more oxygen, fight infection and stop bleeding

LIVER: glycogen is converted into blood sugar to give 'short distance' energy (increase in cholesterol as 'long distance' energy)

SWEAT GLANDS: operate to cool the underlying and overheated muscles

BLADDER & RECTUM: muscles relax to release any excess load

DIGESTION: processes shut down as blood is diverted elsewhere (as a result, the mouth goes dry to avoid adding extra fluids to the stomach)

Figure 6.1 *Alarm reaction*

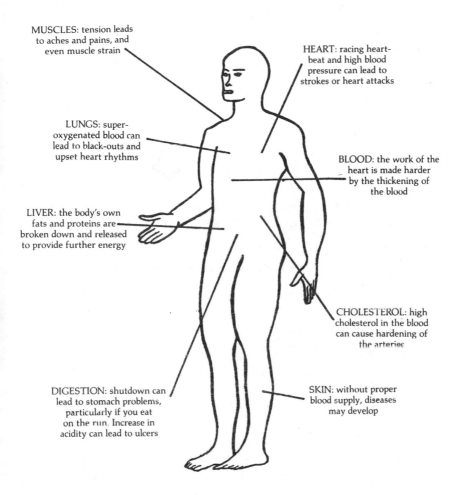

MUSCLES: tension leads to aches and pains, and even muscle strain

HEART: racing heartbeat and high blood pressure can lead to strokes or heart attacks

LUNGS: super-oxygenated blood can lead to black-outs and upset heart rhythms

BLOOD: the work of the heart is made harder by the thickening of the blood

LIVER: the body's own fats and proteins are broken down and released to provide further energy

CHOLESTEROL: high cholesterol in the blood can cause hardening of the arteries

DIGESTION: shutdown can lead to stomach problems, particularly if you eat on the run. Increase in acidity can lead to ulcers

SKIN: without proper blood supply, diseases may develop

Figure 6.2 *Prolonged stress*

What to do

First, consciously work to calm yourself down. If it is difficult emotionally, then work on the physical symptoms directly. Take slow and deliberate breaths. Have a glass of water handy. Make sure the room is ventilated or even go to the bathroom and rinse your face in cold water. Let your muscles relax.

If the stress response is not given proper release (normally through physical action) your body can remain at a heightened level of arousal. Repeated stressful events can 'top up' your stress level and maintain such heightened arousal for a prolonged period. The bodily changes due to prolonged stress are shown in Figure 6.2.

Prolonged stress can be serious. You may need to make important life-style changes. If you think you may have a problem with stress, consult your doctor. In terms of what you can do as part of your own 'health management' we have outlined:

- How to support your body in what you eat and how you eat.
- How to use exercise to release stress and stay healthy.

The cost of stress

The ultimate cost of stress is that your body stops functioning. Like a car which is overworked and denied proper care, it will grind to a halt.

The more subtle cost of stress is that the body does not stop all at once, but that different parts of the body literally take the strain. It may be your skin, or your stomach, or your heart, or even your temperament. Whatever it is, you will perform less effectively, and feel less good physically and psychologically.

The cost of stress does not stop there. The knock-on effects make it more difficult for you to cope. For example, stress can make you irritable and short-tempered. The unhappy consequences of this can be that you turn away potential supporters by the way that you treat them. This can leave you feeling even more pressured than before. From this position, people all too often turn to supports that in the long run do not give support at all. Alcohol is one example of this. In moderation, alcohol can be a great help (in fact, the Maudsley Clinic believes that one glass of wine each day is more beneficial than no alcohol at all). However, as a basis for support it can easily get out of hand and lead to further problems.

So, the cost of stress can be high and you can end up paying this price simply because you have ignored the warning signals sent out by your body. As an international hotel consultant put it: 'If only the last period (of stress in my life) had been a decade later, I would have been more aware that I was stressed and then taken steps to alleviate the situation. Perhaps I would not have had my heart attack.'

Eating for health

Do you treat your body as well as you treat your car?

Your car: Do you put the right grade of petrol in your car? And do you keep the petrol topped up or at least fill it up when the gauge shows 'empty'?

Do you get your car checked when you hear an unusual knocking sound? Most of us probably do these things – they are basic car care. We do them because we want to keep the car running.

Your body: Do you fill up your body with the right grade fuel? Do you stop and fill up when your warning signal says 'I'm hungry!'? Do you work on after all your warning signals say 'Stop'? When you have a headache, when you feel your heart pump, when you hear yourself being irritable and short-tempered with others? Or do you keep going? Heeding these signals is basic body care.

Key point: Your body needs care and maintenance just as much as your car if it is to keep running.

Six rules for a healthy diet

Apart from being generally advisable, healthy eating is part of stress management. A healthy diet may not solve your problems, but it will make your body more resistant to the effects of stress, leaving you with more energy to concentrate on the real issues.

One reason why we need to eat properly, particularly in times of stress, is that under stress the body uses up more energy. A number of the physiological effects of stress (such as thickening blood, rise in cholesterol levels) can also be held in check by sensible eating. For example, drinking adequate water (eight glasses a day) helps to thin the blood, while fibre in your diet acts as a sponge to mop up excess fat and cholesterol.

Here are six things to include in your diet to help you make your body fit to cope with stress:

1. Eat plenty of unrefined foods

Unrefined food is the whole food – with nothing taken out. Whole wheat, for example, is whole food. When it is refined, the bran and the wheatgerm are removed.

Whole and unrefined food can be processed (which means it is mechanically modified by grinding, breaking or heating). For example, whole-grain flour is a processed food, with the whole, unrefined wheat kernel ground into flour. White flour is both refined and processed: something has been removed from the grain and it has been ground as well.

Unrefined whole food has a number of advantages over refined and processed food. Whole food includes essential *fibre*. Fibre assists the process of digestion and is a sure way of correcting constipation.

A high-fibre diet absorbs fats in the digestive system; and it has recently been demonstrated that eating oat bran reduces the cholesterol level of the blood. Fibre also slows down the rate at which the stomach digests food. This means that instead of being hungry again soon after a meal, you will feel full for longer. It also means that your stomach acid works on digesting food rather than attacking your stomach lining. A benefit of this is that it reduces your chance of developing ulcers.

Deriving your sugar from whole food helps to keep your blood sugar level stable. After eating refined sugars your blood sugar

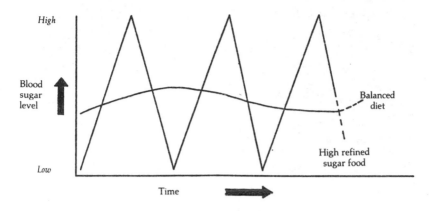

Figure 6.3   *Effects produced on blood sugar level by fast food and drinks with a high sugar content*

level will fluctuate more dramatically, rising quickly then dropping rapidly and producing a desire for more.

You can obtain fibre from a variety of foods, including vegetables (such as beans, peas, corn), whole-grain bread and fruit (an apple a day really can keep the doctor away).

It is worth knowing, however, that calcium absorption can be impaired by a high-fibre diet. This can be easily overcome by drinking a couple of glasses of milk a day (or consuming other foods rich in calcium such as yoghurt and cheese).

2. Keep processing to a minimum

Preparing food can sometimes diminish its nutritional value. Boiling vegetables, for example, removes soluble vitamins and minerals. High heat applied to any foods tends to damage protein.

Foods can also lose value over time. Stored potatoes, for instance, have lost much of their Vitamin C by the end of the winter. Ideally, food should be eaten fresh, with as little processing as possible. A microwave is ideal for cooking vegetables. When you do cook by traditional methods, steam or lightly boil your vegetables. Where possible, use left-over water or juices for gravies and sauces.

3. Be careful about fats

Fats are not actually bad for you. A certain amount of fat is essential in our diet to store energy, protect and insulate body organs, transport vitamins and supply essential fatty acids. However, too much fat, particularly if combined with lack of exercise, can lead to excessive weight gain.

Take fat from a variety of sources (eg animal fats: cheese, eggs, meat; vegetable fats: avocados, peanuts, sunflower seeds).

4. Cut down on sugar and salt

For most of us, the sugar and salt we require is readily obtainable in our diet. It is not necessary to have added sugar and salt, so use them sparingly in cooking and shop for products where these are not added.

5. Vitamins and minerals

Check that your diet gives you a balanced supply of vitamins and minerals. See page 103 for books you might refer to for specialist advice.

In addition to your normal intake, remember that Vitamin B is depleted during stress. If you feel particularly stressed, take a Vitamin B supplement, which can be purchased from chemists or health food shops.

6. Drink plenty of water

The physiological effects of stress include dehydration and consequent thickening of the blood, under-nourishment of the skin and digestive disorders.

To tackle dehydration, increase your intake of liquid. This does *not* mean just drinking more tea and coffee. These are diuretics and actually increase the rate at which liquid is lost. Instead, drink more pure water or natural, unsweetened fruit juice. Experts recommend eight glasses of water a day.

Good hydration assists:

1. blood to thin, preventing damaging clots forming;
2. skin texture to be maintained and body temperature to be regulated through sweating;

3. digestion;
4. washing excess waste products through the body as urine;
5. preventing mucus building up in the lungs and nasal passages (since in dry atmospheres we act as living humidifiers).

Tips for eating out

- If there are vegetarian dishes on the menu, try one of these. They are usually healthier and often very interesting.

- Opt for fresh fruit for dessert rather than a serving of rich sugary pudding from the sweet trolley.

It's not what you eat, it's how you eat it

Eat slowly

Many of us eat too quickly for our own good. If you eat too quickly, you create a sudden load on your stomach. In addition, your body remains 'revved-up', as it were, while you eat. In this heightened state of arousal the digestive system is inhibited. So the more you rush your food, the more problems you deposit in your own system.

If you are not sure how quickly you eat, compare yourself with others. Are you always the first to finish? If so, try taking small breaks while you are eating. Actually place your knife and fork back on your plate for a moment or two. Try to do this at least twice in a meal.

Allow one bite to be fully disposed of before you take the next. Chew your food thoroughly. Most of us rarely chew food properly, leaving the burden of the work to our stomachs. Chewing thoroughly takes longer and slows us down; it also makes things easier on our digestive system.

Eat with someone else

Try to eat with someone else or a group of people. Talking is a great way to slow down eating. The person who talks the most usually ends up finishing last.

If you would rather eat alone, look for other ways to slow down. Why not read a book? Or a newspaper? Or do a crossword? Look for something you find relaxing which will encourage you to pause more frequently during your meal.

Eat regular meals rather than numerous snacks

Snack eating is difficult to monitor and therefore easy to get out of control. Snacks are also notorious for giving a bad balance of vitamins. In many snacks all you really get are empty calories and simple carbohydrates; these are the sorts of foods which will leave you wanting more.

Regular meals, on the other hand, help you to monitor what you eat. And if you can rely on having regular meals, you can be more disciplined about avoiding snacks.

This is not to suggest that you arrange a puritanical regime, just to show that regular meals will lessen the need for snacks. It is when we miss breakfast or work through lunch that we have to make up for it with snack food.

Make it a habit to have breakfast and take your lunch break. And don't forget something in the evening. If you try to save on your evening meal you will probably be hungry later and end up having something just before you go to bed. Eating before retiring at night can lead to indigestion and sleeplessness.

Take a proper break for your food

Consider it an Early Warning Signal that you are under stress if you cannot manage a proper break to eat. Meal times are natural breaks in the day. They provide an opportunity to slow down and take your mind off work. Taking a proper break maximises the usefulness of a meal: you eat better and return to work refreshed and better able to tackle what lies ahead.

If your break must be short, give a little thought as to where you will take it. A change of environment can make even a very short break worthwhile. It removes all the reminders of work and allows you to relax. Try it and you will be more productive when you return.

Sit down to eat

This is a tip many of us can benefit from. Many people eat on the move, or while they are working. They always eat *and do something else* at the same time.

Eat less rather than more

This is another tip that could make many of us more productive, particularly in the afternoon when we hit the 'post-lunch dip' – that drop in performance as we recover from an unnecessarily generous lunch.

The answer is, simply, to eat a lighter lunch. If you know you will be called on to perform later, try to eat in advance. Athletes would not eat before an event – why should you be any different? If your stomach is full and your digestive system working overtime, more of your energy will be diverted to that process. You will have less energy to perform. Give yourself the same consideration as athletes. Eat sensibly and, before major events, eat well in advance.

Take care when using food as a reward

Many of us give ourselves treats or reward ourselves with something special every so often. This is a good idea. Most of us probably do not treat ourselves often enough. A reward is, after all, a great way to reinforce a behaviour pattern we are pleased about.

Food and drink are common sources of reward. We give boxes of chocolates, we have a drink when we celebrate. Because we don't do these things every day, they stand out as special. Yet sometimes we can enjoy the treat so much that we indulge ourselves more and more frequently. This can be the difference between a treat and a bad habit. And a bad habit can easily become a crutch. Is a drink every evening when you arrive home after a hard day a treat or a crutch? It could be either – only you would know.

Clearly, you do not want to worry so much about rewarding yourself that you feel guilty. We should all be prepared to reward achievements or treat ourselves just for the sake of treating ourselves. But why not be a little more imaginative about your treats and rewards? Do they have to be food or drink? What non-consumable treats can you think of?

Non-consumable treats

_____   _____

_____   _____

_____   _____

If you are happy with food- or drink-based treats, how about looking for healthier options? Why not select a piece of your favourite fruit rather than a piece of cake? And why not prevent over-indulgence by going for quality instead of quantity? Instead of a bottle of wine, make it half a bottle of really good wine.

Exercise for stamina, suppleness and strength

How do you feel when you are stressed? Do you feel restless and want to get up and pace about? Have you ever walked down the corridor for a cup of coffee you did not really need? These are all stress Early Warning Signals. Your body is telling you that it is geared up for action. (Conversely, prolonged stress can also make you feel listless and tired.)

What you can do

1. Move about when you feel your level of arousal rising; go for a walk or try to do something else that will use up physical energy.
2. Incorporate a regular routine of exercise into your everday life.

Three kinds of exercise

General rule: Always work within your capabilities. Start off with easy sessions and very gradually move on.

1. Exercise for stamina

Perhaps the most popular kind of exercise, stamina exercises are often enjoyed as games. They are particularly good for releasing pent-up energy. They can also leave you feeling invigorated after a work-out.

What:	Continuous exercises such as aerobics, skipping, running, cycling and swimming. Sports such as squash and tennis are also good but involve more stopping and starting.
Why:	They help you use up oxygen faster and use energy more efficiently.
How and when:	Sessions as little as 15–20 minutes, three or four times a week, plus any time you feel stressed. Check your fitness using the 'talk-test'. Can you talk evenly while you exercise?

2. Exercise for strength

Growing in popularity as people become more aware of their bodies, strength exercises help to keep good muscle tone and release muscle tension.

What:	Greater amounts of work than stamina exercises, for shorter periods. Typified by weight training in the gym, strength exercises can also be done at home: press-ups and sit-ups, for example.
Why:	Help to keep muscles toned for day-to-day use, reducing likelihood of sprains and strains.
How and when:	Repeat each routine a few times but don't push yourself too far. Build up the number of repetitions gradually and then settle on a number you are happy with. Exercise three or four times a week.

A few tips on well-known exercises: keep your knees slightly bent with sit-ups; try press-ups with your knees on the floor if it helps; beginners can do press-ups leaning against a wall. Always start with easy exercises and progress gradually.

3. Exercise for suppleness

This is the most convenient form of exercise. You can do it at home and at work quite easily, concentrating on particular parts of your body that feel tense.

What:	T'ai Chi, yoga or generally rotating joints, stretching, tensing and relaxing muscles or groups of muscles.
Why:	Eases aches and pains caused by muscle tension. Relaxes muscles so that they are less susceptible to muscle tension in the future.
How and when:	Stretch slowly, gradually and well within your limits. Do not bounce or jerk the muscle into stretching further as you may easily cause damage. Instead, concentrate on the feeling of relaxation. Allow breathing to become slow and rhythmical.

Exercise regularly every morning and/or every evening, but don't restrict muscle care to formal times. Stretch, tense and relax muscles whenever they feel tight or before any major physical exertion.

The value in 'having a cigarette'

Smoking is physically unhealthy. However, giving up smoking can also mean giving up an activity which supports you. How this works for you depends on your smoking habits. 'Stopping for a smoke' often becomes a little ritual in itself; it becomes more than the action of merely reaching for a cigarette. You may also take the opportunity to put aside your work for a minute or two and take a break. You light up the cigarette and do nothing else at all.

On a stressful day, these breaks can be very therapeutic. They are often the times when creative people have their best ideas.

But take away the cigarette (or pipe, or cigar) and might you not feel a little foolish or guilty just sitting doing nothing? This is the value of smoking: it provides an acceptable excuse to take a break. So, if you are giving up smoking, don't give up the breaks as well. You will just make it harder on yourself if you do.

Give up the drug, but preserve your rituals as support activities. Instead of 'stopping for a smoke', stop for a micro-break (see page 67) or stop and have a drink or eat a piece of fruit. Whatever it is you do, find a substitute for smoking which allows you to keep your ritual alive.

Tips for healthy living

Smoking

Stop smoking (cutting down has very little effect). Be particularly concerned if you drink as well as smoke: the two have an interactive effect. If you must smoke, do not smoke in front of other people.

Alcohol

A little alcohol is actually good for you. Enjoy a few drinks but avoid excessive consumption. (Two or three pints a week or equivalent is a good target.)

Stop habit-drinking – you get less enjoyment from this anyway. Drink for the taste and when you really want a drink.

Set up non-drinking days.

Keep lunch-time drinking to a minimum.

Look for non-alcoholic drinks you enjoy.

Consider alternatives to drinking.

Pills and potions

Avoid drugs unless absolutely necessary. (Many sleeping tablets, for example, quickly engender some level of dependence.)

If you are prescribed drugs and are concerned about this, ask for a second opinion.

If you do use drugs, keep to the minimum period – try not to go over six weeks without further medical consultation.

Summary

- The stress response prepares your body for imminent action. This is useful in emergencies but causes problems if stress is prolonged.

- Watch out for Early Warning Signals of stress (breathlessness, pumping heart, sweating, muscle aches and pains) and take action directly. Don't wait for these signals; take preventive action now.

- Eat healthier food. Go for more fresh fruit and vegetables but less fat, sugar and salt. Drink plenty of water or fruit juice and monitor your vitamin and mineral intake.

- Develop healthy eating habits. Take proper breaks to eat and don't rush your food. Stop eating *before* you feel full.

- Cut down on poisons to your system such as tobacco, alcohol or caffeine.

- Exercise regularly for *stamina*, *strength* and *suppleness*.

Your points:

_____

_____

_____

_____

_____

_____

_____

_____

Putting it into practice

1. How healthy is your diet? Pick either one thing you would like to *add* to your diet or one thing you would like to *cut down on*. Look through your daily and weekly routine and pinpoint the times when you will make a special effort to make these changes. Note these times in your diary.

2. Identify one unhealthy food or drink you use as a treat for yourself. See if you can think of a healthy alternative that is still a treat. Remember that treats do not need to be food!

3. If you regularly forego a proper eating break, try to stop this habit for one week. Allow at least half an hour for your meal and make it an absolute rule not to do any work during this period. See if your performance goes up or down.

4. Most of us would benefit from treating our bodies to a little more exercise. Choose which type of exercise (suppleness, stamina or strength) you think is right for you. Set yourself a routine to follow and start by doing only half your routine for the first week. (Try to think of everyday activities that can support your routine as well. For example, walk up the stairs instead of using the lift.)

5. Think of ways in which you can *extend* exercise you already take. For example, play squash twice a week instead of once; walk the dog twice round the block, not just once.

Personal Planner	
Key points	*Action to be taken*

Further reading

General texts

The Book of Stress Survival, Kirsta, A, 1986 (Guild)
A very practical book which has a particularly good section on short-term and long-term remedies for stress and deals with health and diet.

The Joy of Stress, Hanson, P, 1988 (Pan)
An easy-to-read paperback. This book covers the whole physiology of stress (including the bodily response, diet and exercise) fairly comprehensively.

Specific texts

The Alexander Technique, Hodgkinson, L, 1988 (Judy Piatkus)
A useful book for those who wish to know more about the Alexander Technique and benefits of correct posture. This is not a 'do-it-yourself' guide to the technique.

Let's Eat Right to Keep Fit, Davis, A, 1986 (Unwin)
A thorough assessment of physical ailments and foods that help well-being.

Nutripoints: The Breakthrough Nutritional Programme, Vartabedian, Dr R E and Matthews, K, 1990 (Grafton)

CHAPTER 7

How to Be Accurate and Positive About Your Performance and Stay in Control

In this chapter, you will learn:

- How to recognise negative thinking
- How to rephrase negative thoughts positively
- How to boost your ego
- How to assess performance fairly
- How to ensure you have your say in an appraisal
- How to handle feelings of helplessness
- How to gain control of your life

Why worry?

You are either ill or you are not ill. If you are not ill there is no need to worry. If you are ill you will either live or you will die. If you live there is no need to worry. If you die you will either go to heaven or you will go to hell. If you go to heaven there is no need to worry. If you go to hell you will be so busy shaking hands with friends that you won't have time to worry.

Anon

How to think positively

Marcus Aurelius, the philosopher and Roman emperor, wrote in his *Meditations* that 'Our life is what our thoughts make it.' So, positive thinking is a way of making your life more positive; it is a way of seeing things that support you, rather than pull you down. It is important since it is as easy to think negatively as to think positively. Henry Ford knew this and summed it up when he said: 'Whether you think you can or you think you cannot, you are absolutely right.'

The first step in positive thinking is to recognise negative thinking. As a rule of thumb, negative thinking takes a fair assessment of a situation and downgrades it, one way or another. We have all done this. Take a look at the examples below and see which ring true for you.

What we say to ourselves	What we are doing
'Oh, I was lucky, anyone could have done it.'	Downgrading achievement.
'It was all my fault.'	Personalising faults (taking the blame).
'I'm useless.'	Generalising faults.
'This is going to be a disaster.'	Exaggerating failure.

Positive thinking is not blind optimism, rather it is a way of reappraising things in order to emphasise the positive. All the above statements could be reworded more positively.

Positive statement	*What we are doing*
'It went very well.'	Accepting achievement.
'Not pressing the blue button was my mistake.'	Accepting responsibility for specific errors.
'I am not skilled in this particular task.'	Specifying areas of competence.
'The potential consequences of this are both good and bad. The good are . . .; the bad are . . .'	Assessing outcomes fairly.

Five rules for positive thinking

1. Accept achievement

If you have done well, recognise this. We can be all too quick to feel bad about our failures, so why not feel good about our successes? Accept credit when it is due. A good way to accept credit without being big-headed is simply to say 'Thank you' and leave it at that. (See also page 51 for more on handling praise and criticism.) If you are not sure whether credit is really deserved, investigate further. Compare what you have done with what others have done. Ask friends or colleagues for an objective assessment.

2. Deal in specifics not generalities

We all do at least one thing badly. The key is not to generalise and let poor performance in one area make others seem sub-standard. Unfortunately, it is easy to allow something small to seem bigger than it is unless we define it very precisely. For example, a child at school might become disillusioned because he or she is 'just no good at maths'. More specifically, this might translate as, 'I find it difficult to do long division and multiplication'. Specifying the problem both defines it (should we decide to tackle it) and limits it (so we don't feel generally incompetent).

3. Realistically assess the chances of your worst fears happening

Work out what a reasonable answer would be. Has it happened before? What circumstances need to come together for it to happen? If it was someone else worrying, would you think that they were being unnecessarily anxious or that their concerns were in all probability quite fair?

> *'My life has been full of terrible misfortunes most of which never happened.'*
>
> Montaigne, 17th-century French philosopher

4. Imagine the worst possible scenario

This is a simple technique to use when you find yourself worrying that something might not go as well as you would like. Imagine the worst possible scenario as a direct challenge to your fears. Ask yourself calmly, 'What is the very worst that can happen?' If you can come to terms with this, you no longer have a problem. You can say, 'OK, I would rather XY happened but if it doesn't, it won't be the end of the world.' The next step is to say, 'What can I do that would make the outcome a little bit better?' Once you begin to concentrate on actions, you won't have time to dwell on your worries.

Remember: What is the worst that can happen?
What can I do that would make the outcome a little bit better?

5. Do your best, then resign yourself to whatever happens

Sir John Harvey-Jones told us that this was something he did. When faced with a problem, he would do everything he possibly could. Then he would face any outcome, even a total crisis, knowing that he had done all that could have been asked of him.

Positive thinking is not a one-off solution. You will get the most out of positive thinking if you persevere until that way of thinking becomes a habit.

'If at first you don't succeed, try, try, try again.'

Proverb

Further thoughts on positive thinking

Aim for something definite

What causes more worry than anything else is uncertainty. Not knowing whether or not you will make a meeting on time is far more worrying than the certainty that you will be late. Once you are certain that you will not make it, you cease to worry and can start thinking about how to make the best of the situation. In your stress management, therefore, you need to aim for something definite. Don't let things slide. For example, if what you are uncertain about is whether or not you will get promotion, ask your manager the criteria on which this will be judged. Then you will have something definite to work towards.

Put negative thoughts into context

Ask yourself, 'Will this matter in six months' or a year's time?' It can also help you to put your problems into perspective if you list all the things you actually have going for you. For example:

- I'm alive.
- I'm healthy.
- I have somewhere to live.
- I have friends.
- I have food in the house.

Your list:

-
-
-
-
-

Once you realise all the things you have (that many others probably do not) you will find your negative thoughts don't seem so numerous and unmanageable after all.

Don't expect too much from positive thinking

Sometimes we feel down for no apparent reason. There may be no negative thoughts to challenge. The way to use positive thinking in these circumstances is to say to yourself, 'This is natural and it is only temporary.' Everybody's self-esteem ebbs and flows like the tide. The purpose of stress management is to help us to appreciate this and to live with it – not to create an artificially permanent high tide.

Concentrate on what is right rather than what is wrong

Dale Carnegie in his book *How to Enjoy Your Job and Your Life* suggests that many of us become unhappy when we concentrate on the 10 per cent of things in our lives with which we are dissatisfied. We are too ready to overlook the 90 per cent of good things. If you think that you do this, try listing your one main worry and then list nine positive points to redress the balance.

Ask yourself, 'Why does this worry me?'

Sometimes we can worry about something without ever really getting to the bottom of why we are worried about it. What we are distracted by may well be a symptom and not the cause of our trouble. So, when you feel pressured, try this: write down what is worrying you, then write down why. Think about this and see if you can work out anything you can begin to do about the real cause of your worries.

How to boost your ego

Publicise your successes

Some people hide their light under a bushel; this is the opposite extreme to boasting and usually makes problems worse.

'Though modesty be a virtue, bashfulness is a vice.'

Proverb

Publicising your successes is a way to ensure you are given the credit you deserve. It also reminds you to feel good about yourself. This is what you do:

- Tell people what you do well rather than what goes wrong.
- When you introduce yourself, detail some of your achievements.
- Explain the obstacles you had to overcome in order to succeed.
- Explain the significance of each success in personal or organisational terms.

It is important not to exaggerate. If you are seen as boasting, people will not only find it distasteful, they will take what you say 'with a pinch of salt'.

Celebrate your successes

Having a celebration is a great way to publicise success. People almost always want to know what you are celebrating and usually like to add their own congratulations. Parties (even low-key gatherings) are particularly good ways to celebrate because you can mingle, enjoy yourself and publicise your success at the same time. But you don't have to have a party: taking your colleagues out or buying drinks or cakes for the office are equally good ways of celebrating and they publicise your success as well.

Give yourself rewards

Giving yourself a party is one way of saying 'Well done' to yourself, as well as involving others in your success. But don't be afraid of giving yourself private rewards as well. The praise we give ourselves is often more meaningful than praise from others.

Give yourself treats

Treats are different from rewards. Treats are something extra – something we give ourselves just for being ourselves, not for any particular accomplishment. People with high self-esteem tend to treat themselves more often than people with low self-esteem. So, if you haven't given yourself a treat in a while, try it. See how much better you feel afterwards.

List your good points

This is a particularly good way of boosting your ego if you are feeling down. However, if you are feeling really low, you may find your good points hard to spot. Why not make your list when you feel good about yourself and then refer to it when you need it. When you make your list, consider:

- What do you most like about your personality?
- What sorts of things do you do better than most people?
- What skills do you have that you are most proud to have developed?
- What is the hardest thing you have accomplished in your life?
- What are you most proud of in your life?

Record your achievements

This is a way of boosting your ego day to day. Often a day or even a week can go and when you look back at it, you think, 'What did I accomplish?' You can get round this problem by simply recording achievements, however small. For example:

- 'I listened attentively to what she had to say without interrupting.'
- 'I limited myself to two drinks after the meeting on Thursday.'

Remember, you are the best judge of your own achievements. Is this something you are pleased to have done? Is it something you would not previously have expected from yourself?

Recording achievements like this is a bit like regularly putting a bit of money to one side for your savings. When you check after only a short time you can be surprised at how much you have accumulated.

How to get a fair and accurate assessment of performance

Balance every negative point with a good point

The purpose of any appraisal (your own or someone else's) is to look at the *whole* performance. This means recognising strengths as well as areas for development. Let's get away from calling these needs weaknesses: weakness implies something that can't be changed, like a weak heart, for example. An area of development clearly signifies that something can be done about it.

Sometimes, however, the good points are taken for granted and only the bad points (the things we want to change) are highlighted. A good way to make you (or your appraiser) think a bit more about the feedback is to adopt the rule: try to balance each negative point with a positive point. However many negative points there are, this rule should ensure that praise for good performance is not left unsung.

Use constructive criticism

This is an important rule for making criticism a positive experience. When you criticise yourself, or when someone criticises you, (a) specify what is wrong and (b) say what can be done to improve the situation. Without this information the criticism is merely an attack, a venting of displeasure; with this information, criticism is something you will welcome as a way of taking your performance forward.

Criticise the behaviour not the person

Teachers are taught to do this. Instead of saying, for example, 'You are an unkind boy, Johnny', a teacher might say 'It was unkind to pull Rachel's hair.'

Concentrating on the behaviour does two things: it forces your criticism to be specific and it shows that the condemnation is centred on what the person has done, not the person himself.

Examples:

Say this:	Not this:
'Telling John that in front of the others was insensitive.'	'You are insensitive.'
'Not asking for other people's views on that issue was inconsiderate.'	'You really are an inconsiderate person.'
'The way you talk in front of the others is often aggressive and overbearing.'	'You are loud and overbearing.'

Try wording criticism this way for yourself as well as for others. You will find that it makes the criticisms easier to accept and respond to.

Share failures as well as successes

Sharing times when things go wrong is a great way to show that we are all human. It is comforting to know that a colleague has made the same mistake as you, or felt the same uncertainty in similar circumstances. When these things are not shared, we lose that reassurance. We can begin to think, 'I bet this hasn't happened to any of them.' From there, it is a short step to attributing the blame to a personal inadequacy rather than accepting it as just one of those things that can happen to anyone once in a while. If you find yourself uncertain about your competence, ask your colleagues if they have ever been in a similar situation. How did they feel? What did they do? What was the outcome?

Show an awareness of the things you need to improve

If someone else is to appraise your performance, ask if you can give your own assessment first. In this way, you ensure that your side of the story is given a proper hearing. It will also demonstrate that you can give a fair and accurate assessment, showing an awareness of the areas you need to improve. This method also benefits the appraiser: the tone of the appraisal is set as a two-way communication between mature adults, rather than an end-of-term report from the teacher. And the appraiser is more clearly aware of how the appraisee sees things and why.

Recognise that in each mistake there is also a lesson to be learned

This can help you to look back at mistakes in a positive light, whether they are your mistakes or mistakes made by anyone else.

How to regain control

Ask yourself, 'How would it be if things were just a little better?'

This is what modern counsellors are taught to ask their clients (see *The Skilled Helper*, Egan, listed on page 119). It is a good way of accepting that while, ideally, there is a lot I would like to change, I can begin with something that just makes things a *little bit better*.

Find out if there is anything you can do

Being out of control is the feeling that 'Whatever I do, it will not make any difference.' A psychologist named Seligman called this 'learned helplessness'. If there really is nothing you can do, then accepting the situation is your only option. Remember that Sir John Harvey-Jones does this – he does what he can and then accepts whatever happens. 'Helplessness', however, is something more than acceptance. It is often an irrational feeling which we can challenge. The way to do this is to break down the individual problems with which you are faced (do not try to tackle them as one) and, for each of them, ask yourself:

(a) What can I do about this?
(b) What can the organisation (or somebody else) do?

You will find that for most issues there is something that both parties can do. While you may immediately make a start on the things you can do, why not also let your manager have a copy of your list? Let your manager know that you are doing your bit – and ask him or her to suggest what is to be done about the other things?

Reduce your expectations when you are stressed

Since so much of stress results from our anticipation that things will not work out, we give ourselves a far greater chance of success if we lower our expectations. This can be doubly effective for, while we can feel stressed if we anticipate failure, we can feel stimulated by a challenge we expect to be able to meet. So, try lowering your expectations when you are stressed. Give yourself a target you know you can hit.

Rehearse your performance like an actor

An actor never goes on stage without going over every detail of his performance beforehand – and doing it several times. Is there any sound reason why we should not give ourselves similar consideration? In fact, many business meetings have a lot in common with acting. Your audience may be smaller, but possibly all the more attentive and potentially critical because of its vested interest. While a major meeting is an obvious stressor, any potentially stressful event is worth a rehearsal. Try this with just one thing over the next week and see how much more confident and in control you feel.

Remember that it is not the situation that is stressful but the way you choose to see it

It is within your control to see something as a pressure or not as a pressure. Recognise that you have this control and try to put it into practice.

Summary

- Practise positive thinking. If you tend to accentuate the negative in your assessment of things, try looking for the positive instead. Remember the words of Marcus Aurelius: 'Our life is what our thoughts make it.'

- Never miss an opportunity to boost your ego. Celebrate your successes, publicise your achievements. Be prepared to tell yourself and others when you have done well and deserve credit.

- When you appraise performance, remember that a pat on the back for good work is as important as criticism for poor work. When you do give criticism, be specific, concentrate on the behaviour not the person and recognise that we all need to make mistakes to help us to learn.

- Regain control of your worries by concentrating on what you can do about them, even if it just makes things a little bit better. If there is nothing to be done, accept the situation as best you can and concentrate on what you will do to make the most of your new circumstances.

My points:

_____

_____

_____

_____

_____

_____

_____

Putting it into practice

1. Think of three ways in which you can celebrate an achievement. Select one of these ways for something you will achieve this week. Try it out and record anything that helps you to improve it next time.

2. Think of three things you would like to achieve over the next week. Select an appropriate reward for each. When you are successful, take pleasure in giving yourself the reward as promptly as possible after the event.

3. List treats you can give yourself. Remember that a treat is anything that you personally find enjoyable or rewarding. Set yourself the target of giving yourself just one of these treats this week. Mark this down in your diary. Try to establish a treat for every week.

4. Draw up a list of your personal and career achievements and have them typed up if possible. Put a copy in your diary for regular reference. Pin up another copy in a place where you will see it every day. When the review date arrives, add any further achievements you have accomplished to the list.

Personal Planner

Key points	Action to be taken

Further reading

How to Stop Worrying and Start Living, Carnegie, D, 1989 (Cedar Books)
> This book is based largely on real instances of how people overcame worry in their lives. It includes interesting insights into the experiences of subsequently successful people.

The Skilled Helper (2nd edition), Egan, G, 1962 (Brooks/Cole)
> This is a book on counselling skills and is worth looking at if your task is to help someone else to come to terms with their problems and take any necessary action. (Michael Reddy's book *Counselling at Work* is also very useful in this respect.)

Staying OK, Harris, A and Harris, T, 1985 (Pan)
> Another book giving practical advice. Although this is based on Transactional Analysis, many of the points stand alone and are suitable for any approach.

CHAPTER 8
How to Build, Use and Give Support

In this chapter, you will learn:

- How to recognise when you are over-reliant on one or two supports
- How to identify other supports you can use
- How to get the most effective balance of supports
- What to do to support yourself
- How to support others

Support mapping

Stress management is simply about ways and means of supporting yourself. We all have and use a great variety of supports. The best copers among us tend to have more supports than others and make more active use of these supports.

What is a support?

A support can be virtually anything. It could be a friend, a technique (such as a method of time management) or a way of behaving (such as assertiveness). The only requirement of a support is that you use it and find it helpful.

Your supports

You can get a clearer picture of the supports you use by drawing a support map. Simply start by writing your name in the centre of a blank piece of paper, then note round your name all the supports you could use (see Figure 8.1).

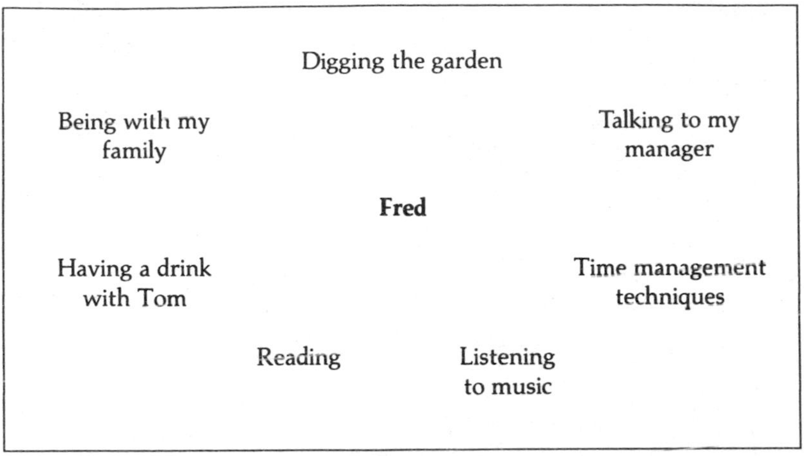

Digging the garden

Being with my
family

Talking to my
manager

Fred

Having a drink
with Tom

Time management
techniques

Reading

Listening
to music

Figure 8.1 *Fred's support map*

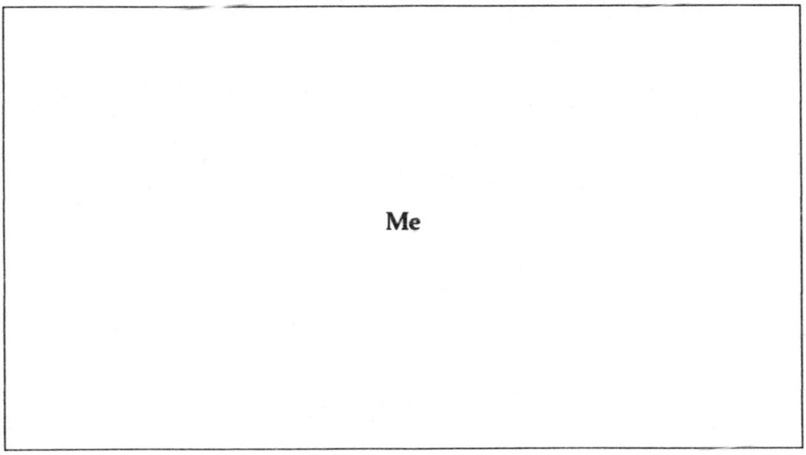

Me

Your map

Draw lines linking yourself to those supports you *actually* use on a fairly regular basis. If it helps to make the map clearer, draw thick lines to the supports you use the most and dotted lines to supports you turn to only occasionally.

Making the most of your support map

Your support map can help you to identify any supports on which you rely too much and any you might use more. To make the most of your support map, draw up an action plan for how you will build up one of your under-used supports.

Once you have written your own support map, ask yourself, 'What can I do to ensure I take greater advantage of any of these supports?'

Getting more out of your support map

This is surprisingly easy to do and there are two techniques to help you. These are the two stress triangles (Figures 8.2 and 8.3).

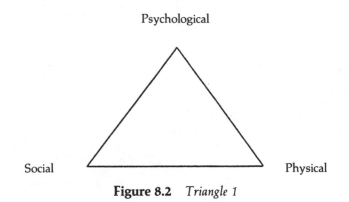

Figure 8.2 *Triangle 1*

Each pressure in your life has three aspects: social, psychological and physical. To illustrate how this works, imagine that your chief pressure is work overload – having too much to do in the time available and with the resources at your disposal. Is this pressure social, psychological or physical?

It is all three.

Socially, you are becoming increasingly cut off. You take work home and are just not able to participate in your usual social life.

Psychologically, you begin to feel burdened. You have so much on your mind you find it difficult to switch off.

Physically, you are run down. You seem to have less energy somehow but also have difficulty getting a full night's sleep.

You therefore experience pressure socially, psychologically and physically. It follows then that in your stress management you should have social, psychological and physical supports.

See how this works using a support map. Choose one source of pressure for yourself and draw your support map for that pressure. Do you have social, psychological and physical supports? If not, try to build in those parts of the triangle you are missing.

Me

Some supports that could be relevant to the example include the following:

Social
- Arrange to see friends one night a week on a regular basis.
- Restrict the number of nights you will bring work home.

Psychological
- Learn and apply time management techniques.
- Find out more about ways of relaxing.

Physical
- Take up a sport or aerobic exercise and practise it regularly.
- Eat regularly and maintain a healthy diet.

The second stress triangle deals with when you use your supports or stress management techniques.

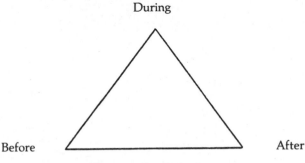

Figure 8.3   *Triangle 2*

You are likely to have a number of supports you can use *after* a stressful event; most people do. Many of us are familiar with the idea of doing something to wind down after the event. Unfortunately, this is often as far as our stress management goes.

The trick to effective stress management is to have supports you can use *before*, *during* and *after* the pressure situation. Think about this for one source of pressure and draw your support map opposite.

Me

Some supports you might have considered include:

Before
- Take a few deep breaths.
- Rehearse what will happen.
- Decide how you can use your choice of clothes and the way you make your entrance to make the most impact.
- Target one thing you will try to do well.
- Remind yourself of past successes.

During
- Slow down your breathing.
- Take a 5–10 second micro-break to compose yourself.
- Concentrate on the one important thing you targeted in advance as a key objective.
- Distinguish between fact and interpretation; what is definite?

After
- Write out what went well, what you learned and what you will do differently next time.
- Go for a walk.
- Find someone to talk you through a debriefing session.

Summary: Support mapping

- The more supports you have the better equipped you will be to handle problems.
- Drawing your support map helps to show you the supports you have (or could have).
- Look for social, psychological and physical supports.
- Look for supports you can use before, during and after stressful events.

Thirteen ways of building support

There are three main sources of support. These are:

(a) supporting yourself
(b) supporting other people
(c) support from other sources.

Supporting yourself

1. Your most important source of support is yourself

If you are determined to undermine yourself, all the outside support in the world will not help you. You must support yourself and a good way to begin is to practise thinking positively.

You may find it helpful to look through Chapter 7 on page 104 for some advice on positive thinking. However, one aspect of positive thinking is so obviously relevant, we will repeat it here. It is how you assess a situation. Ask yourself these three questions:

(a) What is it I am worried about?
(b) What is the worst that can happen?
(c) What can I do?

If you are honest, your answers to these questions will quickly sum up the situation. They will not hide bad news but they will not exaggerate the problems either. They will help you to assess things accurately and gauge what action needs to be taken.

This way of thinking things through helps to stop worry. It is a sure way to support yourself when you feel caught between sensible concern and outright anxiety and despair.

2. Support yourself in what you say

This is a kind of self-encouragement or self-brainwashing, depending on your viewpoint. It has been used most effectively by top sports professionals. One famous golfer says to himself quietly, 'This will go in the hole', just before he attempts a putt. He is not always right, but the positive attitude he engenders helps him to carry on when the going gets tough.

What words of encouragement can you say to yourself in times of crisis? If you find it difficult to know what to say, try thinking back to previous successes and relating them to your present dilemma. For example:

'I overcame the problem in July, I will overcome the problem now.'

'I was appraised as the best person in the department – however this goes, I know I am good at my job.'

3. Develop habits that support you

The way to start is to work out which things are your strengths and which cause you pressure or concern. Two or three strengths and two or three areas of concern are enough to begin with.

Choose one strength and one area of concern and decide on a single habit for each of these: a single thing that, habitually done, will support your development in that area. For example, you might be concerned about not always getting things done, especially leaving important jobs untackled for too long. You might decide to build up the habit of writing a 'To do' list every day.

Or if preventing yourself being overly sharp or aggressive to others was a concern, you could set up a habit of stopping for five seconds before responding when you felt annoyed, and saying to yourself under your breath, 'He/she could be right.'

This book gives many tips on habits you could adopt. Choose one or two to begin with and build these into your routine to support you. They will soon become 'second nature' and you can concentrate on the next point you want to improve.

4. Break habits which bring you trouble

Over-eating, smoking and excessive drinking are common habits that people want to break. Unfortunately, what makes habits such good supports is that they can be difficult to break once established. Difficult, but not impossible.

Your doctor will probably be able to give you good advice on breaking the habits mentioned above, but as an extra guide, here are some general tips for habit breaking:

How to break habits

- Draw up a contract with yourself (or someone else if it is more helpful), detailing your expected progress and the rewards you will earn.

- Imagine what it will be like to break the habit. Visualise the good and the bad. Tell someone else how you think it will be.

- Do a trial run. Break the habit for a short time. Was it as bad as you predicted?

- Once you have stopped the habit, try not to slip back. It will be twice as hard next time.

- Don't let yourself suffer for breaking the habit. Choose an acceptable reward and make sure you give yourself the reward regularly to reinforce your progress.

Support from other people

5. Seek support from other people

From personal friends to professional counsellors, it is other people who win the popular vote for supports. If you agree that people are important in this way, ask yourself, 'How extensive is my personal network?'

Who could you turn to about:

- financial worries?
- personal problems?
- work difficulties?
- health concerns?

If appropriate, break down your work into areas. Who can you turn to if problems arise in these areas?

If you are satisfied with the names you have thought of, you can feel pretty reassured. If not, then set out to build a network of people who can support you. And remember, support is not confined to emotion; it includes practical help and advice as well.

6. Build alliances

'Networking' is the jargon for building and using contacts. Networking is trendy and in some circles it is almost a source of one-upmanship to list how many contacts you have in your network.

Support is much more than this. Where networking is about contacts, support is about building *alliances*, developing relationships.

Strive to get to know your contacts. What are their interests and values? What do they know about you? What can you do for them as a first step towards a stronger alliance? If you find it helpful, list the names of chosen contacts and your answers to these questions.

7. Try talking to a counsellor

A counsellor is a support used by more and more people in Britain. To benefit from seeing a counsellor, however, it helps to consider the point of view that 'Counselling is for wimps'. If you genuinely believe this, the chances are that you won't go to a counsellor anyway; and if you do, you probably won't listen a great deal.

But counselling is not confined to wimps. Nor is it just about problems. The time to see a counsellor is often when you feel your best – when you are on top of the world, without a problem in sight. If you do this, counselling helps you to build on what you already have. It is a true support, just like the foundation of a building. It is not there just so that things don't fall down – it is the basis upon which to build further.

Support from other sources

8. Anything can be a support

If you have a lucky charm, why not use it? If it helps to allay your fears or makes you feel more confident, it is a good thing. Many of us have such lucky tokens. Even if, deep down, we don't really believe them, they can still bring the reassurance we need. The most decorated American soldier in Vietnam, Colonel D Hackworth, reported that almost every soldier in his command had his equivalent of a 'comfort blanket'. For some it was a rabbit's foot, for others an article of clothing – but whatever it was, it made them feel better, more confident.

Be careful, however, that your 'comfort blanket' does not work against you. How do you feel if you do not have it with you? Anything that makes us unnecessarily superstitious can end up causing more harm than good. So by all means have your own 'comfort blanket', but don't be dependent on it. If there is something you can do in addition, then do it. As the saying goes: 'Trust in Allah but tie up your camel.'

9. Remember that 'You are what you wear'

Clothes are an underrated source of support. Even when you feel slightly lacking in confidence, the right clothes can bolster your feelings and enhance your image.

Wearing a favourite jacket, for example, can help you to feel more confident. And the right clothes support you in terms of what others see, even if beneath them you are still a little unsure of yourself. Remember to use clothes as a part of your body language that has an immediate impact.

10. Use hobbies and routines to support yourself

Many of us do this anyway. For example, 'Digging the garden' is a common reply when managers asked what helps them when they feel stressed. If it isn't digging the garden for you, it could be any of a legion of hobbies and activities.

In fact there are so many different possibilities that it is useful to classify them into different groups. It will then be easier to see for yourself if you are making the most of the possible supports around you.

One classification is HAIR. This stands for:

Hobbies
Activities
Interests
Rituals

These are explained below:

Hobbies
Do you have a hobby you can lose yourself in? Gardening, fishing and all kinds of sports are common examples, but the range of possible hobbies is enormous. A fully-fledged hobby is a good counter-balance to working life and can help you to keep your perspective when work concerns seem overwhelming.

Activities
Are there any particular activities you enjoy? These are not really fully-fledged hobbies (although the dividing line is not necessarily that distinct), but things you do that take your mind off work. A solicitor friend enjoys cooking when he gets home. Sir John Harvey-Jones finds reading is his great escape. He says, 'I need a generous dose of imaginative reading every week.'

Interests
What things would you like to know more about? They could be work-related or they could equally be anything at all. One

manager, for example, recently decided he would like to find out more about Ancient Britain. His school education had mentioned the Celts, Angles and Saxons, but that was all. He resolved to pursue this interest and find out more. This has provided him with a fascinating distraction from work worries and added a whole field of interest to his life.

Choose something you would like to know about and pursue it. When you are satisfied, choose another interest. You will probably become a more interesting person to be with and you will have a more balanced view of your whole life.

Rituals
What rituals do you have in your life? A morning (or evening) walk could be a ritual; or putting aside half an hour at the end of the day to read the paper.

What rituals could you establish?

11. Remember to work, rest and play

If play was banned there would be an uproar, for without play life becomes one long work-rest-work cycle. But notice how easy it is to trick yourself into this depressing routine. A hard day at the office, a tiring journey home and you could be cancelling that planned evening out. It is so much easier to flop down on the settee in front of the TV. Of course, sometimes a night in is a great means of relaxation and a positive choice. At other times, it is the result of finding reasons not to do something instead of reasons for doing it. Paul Mathews, Assistant Director for Engineering, British Gas South East, has a rule which enables him to ensure he makes the most of his available leisure time. The rule is this: even if he feels tired and wants to give in to the urge to 'flop down', he will press on for at least five minutes. Nine times out of 10 he will forget his tiredness as he becomes absorbed in the new activity. Overall, the rule has meant his enjoying countless activities he would otherwise have missed.

'. . . the purpose of life must be more than going to work, coming home and going to bed.'

Bob Geldof, pop star and author

12. Recognise pets as a source of support

In some ways, animals are the best of supports because they don't sit in judgement over you. While relationships with people often blow hot and cold, relationships with animals are more reliable.

There is even scientific evidence to back up the benefit of 'pet support'. A recent report revealed that dog-owners suffered less from headaches, backaches, sleeplessness, colds and 'flu, as well as enjoying substantially better mental health. One international hotel consultant finds support from animals and says his two horses are 'a great help'.

One reason why pets help is that simply caring for them can stop us looking inward at our own problems.

13. Have a place where you can relax

Many people have favourite places. One man who lives near Woodstock likes to walk around the extensive grounds of Blenheim Palace every so often; or at other times to drive the car to the top of a hill overlooking the countryside. For him these places are peaceful and he is able to think matters through when he goes to them.

Do you have any special places you can go? Do you make as much use of them as you might?

How to give support

Here are five ways of checking how well you support others.

1. See how you can contribute to another person's support map

If your job involves managing other people, consider what role you play (or could play) in their support maps. How approachable are you? Do others know they can turn to you? What kind of help could you supply? (Remember that as a manager you might be a link to other supports such as training, improved facilities, extra resources, feedback on performance.)

Try not to disrupt other people's support maps. When you

have an office reshuffle or you re-allocate duties, see whose support maps you might be affecting. A changed routine, for example, could mean that Joe can't meet his friends for lunch in the pub any more; or that Pat can't make her evening classes. Two managers explained how both their support maps had been hit when one of them was seconded to another office. Previously, they had been each other's chief supports so, with the secondment, both of them lost that support. They still carried out their jobs, but the change would have been much easier to handle if their boss had only realised how much support he was taking away.

2. Be a supporter, not an empty reassurer

True supporters accept that there is a problem and move straight on to what help can be given. True supporters say, 'I can see this will be difficult for you'; 'You have a right to be concerned about this'.

Empty reassurers, on the other hand, try to brush problems away or pretend they don't really exist. They say, 'It'll be all right'; 'Don't worry about it'.

There is nothing worse than being told a problem is not serious if you know it is, or to be told to stop worrying when you are already very concerned. The first step in being a true supporter is to face facts and accept that the issue is a problem (or at least, a problem for that person).

3. Offer practical support

Supporters try to define how they can help. Supporters will say, 'What do you want me to do?' Or, if the person needing help is too worried to think straight, 'This is what I can do – will that help?'

Empty reassurers never mention practical help.

4. Offer emotional support

This is what empty reassurers claim to do. In fact they are rarely interested in whether their comments are comforting or not.

They do not want to be involved; they just want to make a point about how silly it is for you to get worked up over an issue they could handle easily.

Supporters offer *real* emotional support. They make themselves available should you need to talk things through. Sometimes this constant availability is enough on its own. Supporters are clear about their support, making it explicit by saying things like 'I will be here between two and four every day if you want to call me' and 'I will be with you all the way.' How much do you make your support clear to others?

5. Support people going forward

Supporting people is a positive activity. It is not just about helping people with problems but about helping people to move forward. Ultimately, support is what you give on the way to enabling people to do more for themselves. How much support do you give to people going forward?

The skilled supporter

'Inadequate support and guidance to help me to do my job' was cited as a key pressure for people in the survey we conducted during the development of this material. What could be the reason for this? It could be that managers are so busy themselves that they have little time to give their subordinates the support and guidance they need.

Yet giving support and guidance need not be time-consuming. However, the consequences of inadequate support and guidance – having to go back over a job that is not done properly, having to counsel a subordinate who has lost all confidence – undoubtedly are time-consuming.

Perhaps, then, it is a question of managers being unclear about what is meant by support and guidance; how much help they should give and where to draw the line. In short, how to be a skilled supporter. Here are some dos and don'ts.

Don't:

- Use delegation as a tool to gain you time in the short term; you will only lose it in the long term.

- Offload your unwanted work on someone else in the guise of delegation. There is no surer way of de-motivating people and making them feel undervalued.

- Offload work on someone without clearly explaining both what is expected and how this can be achieved – otherwise you are only setting up a failure.

- Offload work (as above) and then come down heavily when you find it hasn't been done properly. You will merely make the person feel more inadequate or resentful. You should have explained it better at the outset.

- Play 'my way' – that is, interfere with a piece of work or criticise it later only because it hasn't been done exactly how you would have done it. Allow a degree of latitude.

Do:

- Let people know the parameters of their responsibility. Even better, negotiate this with them.

- Specify the end result you want to see. Don't just leave someone with a job – leave them with a clear vision as to what will constitute successful completion. Agree a deadline date.

- Consider how the work will be done. Allow people some flexibility for doing it their way, but specify any resources, finance or authority that are available to them.

- Let people know the consequences they can expect. This includes rewards (such as praise, position, promotion, money, future work) as well as the consequences if the result is not favourable. These consequences are not punishments: they are there to show that there is life after failure. They might include training, trying another similar job, trying something different.

- Establish possible warning signs that both parties can look for in case things aren't going well. If it is a long project, establish milestones to monitor progress.

The essence of good support and guidance is clear communication and known availability. But availability means being there if you are needed – not being there regardless. Give people support, but give them also the space and opportunity to develop.

Summary

- Use a support map to assess your strengths and the areas you can develop in your stress management. Use the two stress triangles to make the most of your support map and redraw your support map once a month.

- Remember that you are your own most important source of support. Support yourself in your 'self-talk' and in your habits.

- Seek support from other people. Build alliances rather than mere contacts; recognise that counselling can be a positive source for development.

- Don't limit yourself in your choice of supports. *Anything* can be a support.

- Support others by listening to what they say, offering practical and emotional support, allowing them the opportunity to develop.

- Remember that support and guidance is rooted in clear communication and known availability. Prevent confusion by specifying the desired outcome, outlining the resources (etc) that can be used and detailing the consequences that can be expected. Agree on how to monitor progress.

Your points:

_____

_____

_____

_____

Putting it into practice

1. List the names of contacts with whom you can build alliances. Keep your new list of 'allies' in your diary. Review your list every month to see if you can add to the list or do something to strengthen one of the alliances you already have.

2. Write down in your diary the times you will set aside for hobbies, activities and the pursuit of special interests. Choose a new interest every month or two to keep yourself on your toes.

3. Choose a single habit you will build into your routine to make yourself more effective. Set yourself a realistic timetable and mark the review date in your diary.

4. Identify a development task you could delegate, then delegate it following the dos and don'ts in this section.

Personal Planner

Key points	Action to be taken

Further reading

Manage Yourself, Pedlar, M and Boydell, T, 1988 (Fontana)
Very much an interactive book, intended for the 'thinking manager'. It includes activities and exercises to help you to get to grips with managing yourself.

The Manager's Guide to Counselling at Work, Reddy, M, 1987 (Methuen)
A practical guidebook for anyone who wants to improve the support they give to others.

A Manager's Guide to Self-Development (2nd edition), Pedlar, M, Burgoyne, J and Boydell, T, 1986 (McGraw-Hill)
A very practical and detailed workbook for self-development.

Further Reading from Kogan Page

Assert Yourself: How to do a good deal better with others, Robert Sharp, 1989

Developing Self-Esteem: A positive guide for personal success, Connie D Palladino, 1990

How To Change Your Life: From thought to action, Antony Kidman, 1989

Managing Your Time, Lothar J Seiwert, 1989

Successful Self-Management: A sound approach to personal effectiveness, Paul R Timm, 1988

Tactics for Changing Your Life, Antony Kidman, 1989